RUG HOOKING JOURNEYS:

Finding the Maker in the Rug

by Tamara Pavich

Presented by
RUG HOOKING

Copyright © 2019 by Ampry Publishing LLC
Published by
AMPRY PUBLISHING LLC
3400 Dundee Road, Suite 220
Northbrook, IL 60062
www.amprycp.com

www.rughookingmagazine.com

Graphic design by Matt Paulson.
Front cover: *The Bright Blessed Days*, designed and hooked by Tamara Pavich.

All rights reserved, including the right to reproduce the book or portions thereof in any form or by any means, electronic or mechanical, including photocopying, recording, or by any information storage and retrieval system, without permission in writing from the publisher. All inquiries should be addressed to *Rug Hooking Magazine*, 3400 Dundee Road, Suite 220, Northbrook, IL 60062.

Printed in the United States of America
10 9 8 7 6 5 4 3 2 1

Photography by the artists unless otherwise noted.
Cataloging-in-Publication Data
Library of Congress Control Number: 2018966561

ISBN 978-1-945550-36-2

CONTENTS

DEDICATION/ACKNOWLEDGMENTS..iv

Introduction..*1*

Chapter I *Self-Reflection in Rug Hooking*....................................*4*

Chapter II *In Honor of Women: Diane Cox*..................................*19*

Chapter III *Myth and Folklore: Ann Willey*..................................*37*

Chapter IV *Symbols and the Self: Håkon Grøn Hensvold*...............*55*

Chapter V *Past, Present, and Future Selves*...................................*80*

Chapter VI *Hooking to Heal*..*98*

Chapter VII *Creating Alter Egos, Characters, and Heroes*..............*111*

CONCLUSION...128

SUGGESTED READING...130

DEDICATION/ACKNOWLEDGMENTS

I am most grateful to every rug hooker featured here, along with my buddies here in the Midwest: Linda Boehle, Terri Bangert, Luci Bolding, Holly McMillan, Jodi Isom, Ann Eastman, Dennie Hoffman, Laurie Christiansen, Karla Egger, Anita White, and Karen Greenfield.

To Deb Smith, thank you for your patience and good advice.

My love and deepest gratitude belong to Lilly Phillips and Mike Pavich, on whom I can always depend.

The idea for this book germinated in 2014 with my discovery of the works of Diane Louise Cox. I was planning my first book of design ideas that encouraged rug hookers to create and draw their own patterns. Rather than using commercial patterns every time, I made a case for reflecting one's own tastes and telling one's own stories. In those chapters, I urged rug hookers to design around color, art, style, or story. The final chapter of *Designed by You* was about designing rugs around ourselves, our own identities. While writing, I pondered the way Diane was hooking some version of her own image into the hessian of nearly every rug, and something in those images spoke to me. Before I had even finished my first manuscript, I was writing the proposal for this book on self-reflection.

Diane signed on right away, bless her, and artists Ann Willey and Håkon Grøn Hensvold graciously accepted my invitation, too. As I reached out to friends, the excitement touched off a flurry of emails and phone calls. I have said that there are three or fewer degrees of separation between all the rug hookers on this earth, and quickly these pages have filled up with interesting and beautiful rugs from the US, the UK, Canada, and Norway.

As I said of my first book about rug hooking, this one too is a trove of original designs, the product of many imaginations. I hope you'll treasure it, as I do.

Detail of Ann Willey's **Ocean Window**. *See the full rug on page 49.*

INTRODUCTION

FINDING THE MAKER IN THE RUG

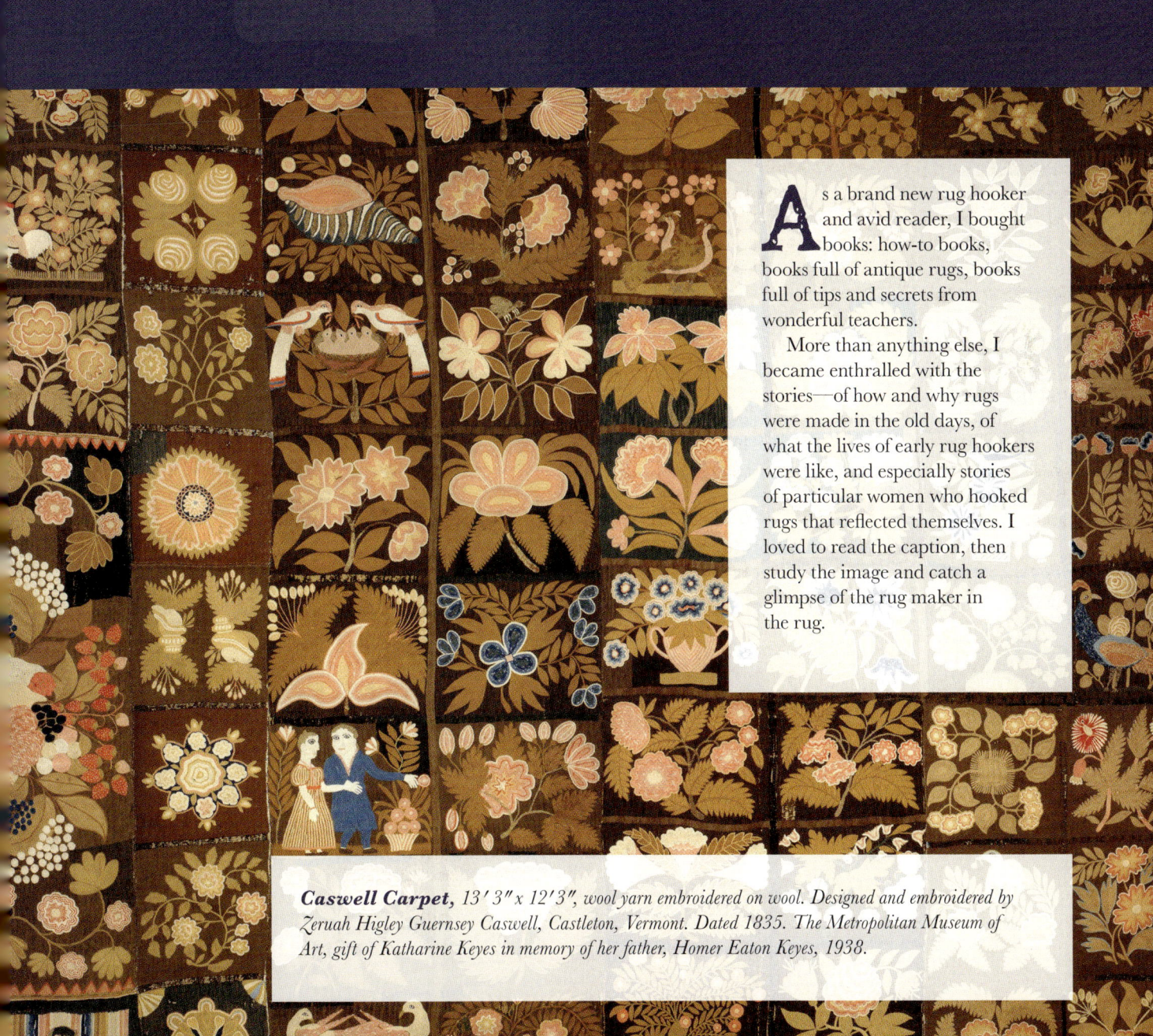

As a brand new rug hooker and avid reader, I bought books: how-to books, books full of antique rugs, books full of tips and secrets from wonderful teachers.

More than anything else, I became enthralled with the stories—of how and why rugs were made in the old days, of what the lives of early rug hookers were like, and especially stories of particular women who hooked rugs that reflected themselves. I loved to read the caption, then study the image and catch a glimpse of the rug maker in the rug.

Caswell Carpet, 13′ 3″ x 12′ 3″, wool yarn embroidered on wool. Designed and embroidered by Zeruah Higley Guernsey Caswell, Castleton, Vermont. Dated 1835. The Metropolitan Museum of Art, gift of Katharine Keyes in memory of her father, Homer Eaton Keyes, 1938.

We may think that the idea of reflecting oneself through rug hooking is something new, but in fact it is as old as the art itself. Perhaps the most well-loved book on rug-hooking history is *American Hooked and Sewn Rugs: Folk Art Underfoot* by folk-art experts Joel and Kate Kopp. In collecting the finest examples for their book, the authors declared, "We believe that to constitute true folk art, a rug must not only have a strong sense of design but also a feeling of feedback from the emotions and sensibilities of the maker."

"The most famous and well-documented masterpiece of American rugmaking," the Kopps wrote, "is the Caswell Carpet, named after its maker, Zeruah Higley Guernsey Caswell. This monumental undertaking in wool tambour embroidery on wool required skill, patience, planning, and an inspired artistic imagination, not to mention years of tedious work."

In her New York Times article "When Home Was Where the Art Was" (June 8, 2007), Roberta Smith revealed a little history behind the Caswell carpet, whose maker devoted three years to shearing the sheep, dyeing and spinning her yarn, and embroidering the entire 12' x 13' rug. Zeruah started this project in 1832, "when she turned 27 and must have seemed on the brink of spinsterhood," Smith wrote. "The desire for a mate is palpable. Note the progress, right to left, of embroideries depicting solitary birds, then pairs of lovebirds, then birds thrusting worms into the mouths of hungry offspring."

Smith also notes a small block of the rug that was of special interest to Joel and Kate Kopp: "The vignette of the young couple arm in arm," the Kopps wrote, "must have had a special significance for Zeruah because for many years she kept it covered with another design sewn on top of it." Happily, Zeruah did finally marry and unveil the happy couple in her rug. According to the Kopps, "she proudly showed it off to visitors throughout her very long lifetime."

With the Caswell carpet, we can look back 184 years to a rug maker quietly—even secretly—sewing her greatest longings into a magnificent work of art. Zeruah Caswell revealed her heart's desire to a point of discomfort, in that she felt compelled to hide her dream of love and marriage until it had come true. She channeled her desires and disappointments into her beautiful rug.

This book is filled with contemporary examples of such makers and such works of art. Our featured artists—Diane Cox of England, Ann Willey of Michigan, and Håkon Grøn Hensvold of Norway—each have their own ways of exploring their identities through their hooked rugs. Thirty more rug hookers from across the country have explored and expressed their identities, allowing readers like us to find them in their finished works.

2 | Rug Hooking Journeys

"Making rugs is a meditative act, pulling fabric through a backing, and thus restoring yourself."
—Diane Cox

CHAPTER 1

SELF-REFLECTION IN RUG HOOKING

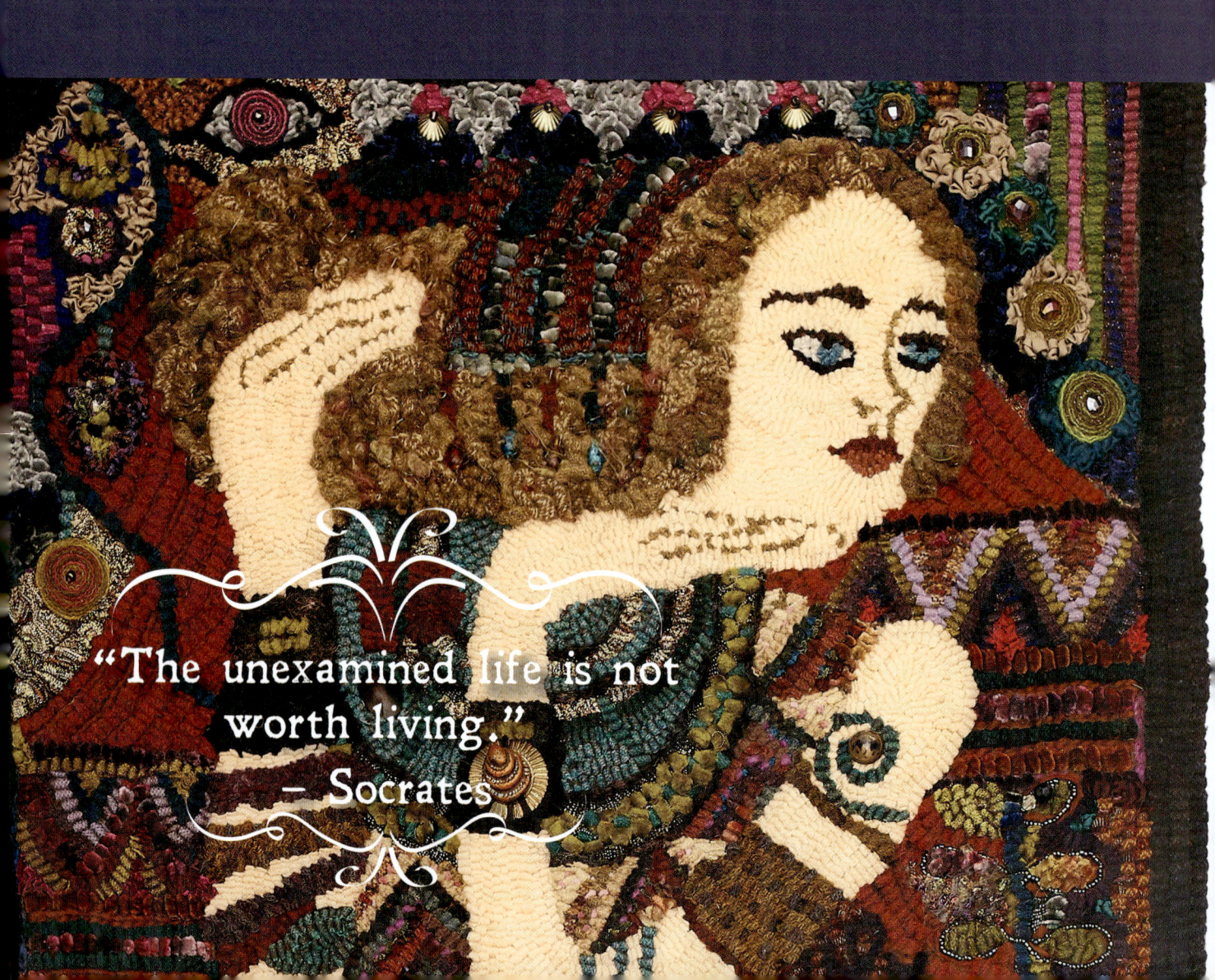

"The unexamined life is not worth living."
— Socrates

Making Self-Reflective Rugs

In the first chapter of his book, *The Illuminated Life*, Abe Arkoff, my late friend who was Professor Emeritus of Psychology at the University of Hawaii at Manoa, suggests that there are three stages of life: youth, mature adulthood, and later life when we may be able to seek a greater understanding of ourselves or perhaps determine a surer sense of purpose and direction. Professor Arkoff's "third age" is less about chronology and more about the consciousness with which we may proceed on our journeys. Those who choose to be self-aware in their third age may pause to get their bearings, re-examine values, look back on turning points in their life stories, and then consider their own potential and goals as they move forward along their paths.

The act of designing and hooking a rug can be very useful to those who seek to examine their own lives. A great deal of rug hooking takes place in solitude, leaving our minds free to reflect on other things. Even when a project requires our concentration, this kind of handwork includes long stretches when our minds may wander at will. "Making rugs is a meditative act," Diane Cox said, "pulling fabric through a backing, and thus, restoring yourself."

In this book, we will explore many kinds of self-reflective rugs. "Art in my life," Ann Willey declared, "seems to be about processing and finding solace." For each rug hooker in these pages, art may serve a different purpose: celebration of life's joys, musing on paths not taken, release from sadness and grief. Art that is born out of experience can endow our lives with meaning and, importantly, help us comprehend and appreciate that meaning.

This book is a study of rug hookers who narrow the lens, whose art involves a personal kind of expression and a meaningful sort of reverie during the making process. The art becomes the medium for depicting and revealing something more of oneself and lending each rug the singularity and uniqueness of its maker. "Rug hooking has become more and more important," Håkon Grøn Hensvold said, "because I feel I have found my medium to tell my stories."

Windows into Other Lives

When I discovered the rugs of Diane Cox—and later, the self-reflective pieces of many rug hookers—I found works that inspire much more than appreciation of beautiful artistry. In studying these rugs and stories, a viewer may join in the maker's reflections, sometimes playfully, sometimes with curiosity, and sometimes somberly. This book is a big collection of windows into other lives.

What do these rug makers allow us to see through these windows? In fact, about a dozen of the rug hookers whose work is featured here have depicted sorrow or injury. These are rugs through which they have attempted to heal or have experienced some kind of renewal or restoration of themselves. Another group has evoked alter egos—other selves—usually with overtones of humor, whimsy, or magic. A large number of makers decided to capture an image of themselves in the past, the present, or even in the future, inspiring reflections on who they are, where they've come from, and the relationships and places that have impacted their characters and identities.

Norwegian teacher and artist Håkon Grøn Hensvold creates large and intricate rugs in which he speaks to his viewer through a language of symbols. Michigan designer Ann Willey weaves myth, archetype, folklore, and fairy tales into her small tapestry-like hookings, finding ways in which classic tales intersect her own life. Diane Cox, our first featured artist, identifies with other women and attempts to honor women by chronicling their stories and plights in her art.

Before we get to our featured artists, we should define this thing we're calling "self-reflection" and distinguish it from other concepts. What is it? What isn't it? Let's begin with some terms and their definitions.

What We Mean by "Self-Reflection" (and What We Don't Mean)

At the outset of this project, we somehow needed to gauge…
- how much a particular design might pique the viewer's curiosity about the maker,
- how widely the image opens a door to the character or story of the person who held the hook and pulled the loops,
- how the design might reveal "the emotions and sensibilities of the maker," as folk-art scholars Joel and Kate Kopp put it.

Since every rug somehow expresses its maker, we needed to differentiate between *self-expression* and *self-reflection*.

Arguably, every rug ever hooked is an example of self-expression. If I hook a commercial pattern of fall leaves, I certainly express myself (to say nothing of my appreciation of fall leaves) in my choices of color, value, intensity, and also through my method and style of hooking. When I design my own rugs, I take self-expression further because I become the creator of every aspect of it—the idea, the pattern, the way it is hooked, and the selection of a color scheme. As designers and as makers, we necessarily express ourselves, consciously or unconsciously.

But to embark on *self-reflection* through rug hooking is a different matter. Most hooked rugs are not examples of conscious self-reflection. In this book, however, we share a trove of widely varied examples of such creations.

Each artist included in these pages explores identity, broadens or sharpens his or her sense of self, works through difficulties, attempts to heal from losses, and/or opens up new ways of thinking about him- or herself. Self-reflection may be whimsical and lighthearted

Puss Crosby, Alter Ego

"After reading Wanda Kerr's amusing way of working out your hooking alter ego name—the name of your very first pet and the name of the first road you lived on—I thought it would be fun for our hooking group to work out our alter egos and hook them," Diane said.

"My alter ego name was Puss Crosby, and I pondered on this name for a long time, especially during my dog walks. Gradually she began to emerge inside my head. I started to make sketches and eventually drew her out quite simply on the hessian. Whilst hooking, I was listening to music and a phrase in Crosby, Stills and Nash's 'Suite: Judy Blue Eyes' seemed to resonate with me: 'How can you catch the sparrow?' So that question was hooked into her. I deliberately wanted the words to appear a bit fuzzy, because Puss was thinking them, not speaking them. The wings came about halfway through, not planned at all.

"Altogether it was a magical experience hooking her. I just let it flow with few expectations. At the end, I realized that she had become very meaningful to me. The sturdy boots symbolize being grounded. The flowers growing up the boots represent a love of nature. The apron means domesticity, and the cat means female intuition. The tiny insignificant bird is a wise old soul, and her wings are freedom and the means of escaping whenever she feels like it."

Puss Crosby, Alter Ego, 26" x 52", a mix of recycled fabrics, knitting yarns, hand-spun wool, sari silk, and a knitted woolen sweater on hessian. Designed and hooked by Diane Cox, Penzance, Cornwall, UK, 2012.

for some artists, serious and thought-provoking for others, even profound and sobering for some. We see self-reflection as a means of deepening the practice of our art and endowing it with greater meaning.

Self-reflection includes the intent and purpose of the art maker. It's usually a conscious effort or inquiry. Self-reflection can be a way of seeking. It asks questions. It imagines and remembers. It ponders and muses. This concept suggests a quest—perhaps an urgent quest—or maybe a relaxed and meditative journey of inquiry. It is motivated by curiosity, by interest. It engages in the process of examining one's own life, as Socrates suggested, and therefore making that life more worthwhile. Such a quest can be whimsical, playful. It could be adventurous or heroic. The goal may be to liberate our spirits. The process moves in the direction of discovery.

Self-reflection is not a symptom of a big, bad ego on the loose. It doesn't require all the hours of the day. It is not selfish or self-absorbed. It need not be heavy or burdensome. It's not a process of psychological analysis (though it could be).

Another way of saying "self-reflection" might be "mindfulness about oneself." Mindfulness is placing our calm attention on something and allowing it to appear more fully to us. For women especially, who may have devoted much time to the care of others, this gentle self-attention could be long overdue. The obligations of family, work, and community often occupy the majority of our waking hours, so when we consciously devote time to self-reflection, we move in the direction of healthy balance. Sometimes it's a balance we truly need.

As we sketch and imagine, we may find that our desires for ourselves surface. Rug designing and hooking is an excellent way to discover the direction we hope to move in our lives and the people we want to become. We might call these people "alter egos" or "other selves," who may or may not be realized.

Jenny Joseph wrote a poem called "Warning," which begins, "When I am an old woman, I shall wear purple, and a red hat that doesn't go and doesn't suit me." This narrator is tired of conforming to other people's rules and customs. She's bored with delayed gratification, sick of holding herself in check and always doing the responsible thing. She longs to "go out in my slippers in the rain/And pick the flowers in other people's gardens/And learn to spit." In this poem, she is exploring an alter ego, a future old woman in a red hat and purple coat, who does what she damn well pleases. Her poem is a form of self-reflection.

Hooked in the spirit of Jenny Joseph's poem "Warning." Turn to page 114 and page 123 for the rugs of Brigitte Webb and Marsha Munter.

Tumbling Cups, *10″ x 15″, recycled fabrics on hessian. Designed and hooked by Diane Cox, Penzance, Cornwall, UK, 2017. "I hooked this rug when I had so much to do it was like spinning plates! So I hooked tumbling cups instead."*

8 | Rug Hooking Journeys

For Women, Especially

For many women of my generation, there hasn't been a whole lot of time for introspection. There was probably even less for our mothers, who had few conveniences and who juggled everything, long before Gloria Steinem and Betty Freidan had made an impact on the culture. Our moms washed cloth diapers, scrubbed on hands and knees, cooked a balanced dinner each night, and put on lipstick before their husbands came home from work.

Our generation grew up with feminism, and we had a lot of modern household appliances and conveniences on our side. We knew it was okay to have a family and a career. Still, it was conventional to direct much of our energy outward, devoting the best of ourselves to loved ones and to certain institutions for whole decades of our lives: raising children; performing and conforming at work; and attending to those salt-of-the-earth, middle class responsibilities to church, to community, to family. When we reach the middle years and nests begin to empty, when ambition has run its course and other busy youngsters are taking over some of those community tasks, that's when we have time to take a breath, pick up a hook, and think about who we are without all those roles that used to define us.

Greater Than Our Roles

Roles are fine, unless they become traps. They can narrow our idea of who we are rather than broaden it. They can make us into conformers or performers. If I've been the head surgical nurse in a hospital for thirty years, I might forget that I was once a daring young girl who kissed a boy behind the cotton candy booth at the county fair. If you spent years in corporate offices, your desire to dig in the garden and plant flowers may have escaped you. The dependable mom and wife of many decades may have neglected the woman with adventure in her heart. We are greater than those roles we have played during the chapters of our lives, and self-reflective art may be just the way to rediscover former or future versions of ourselves.

"What versions?" you might ask. "There's only one me."

Oh, that's where you're wrong. Here's an exercise you can do with a paper and pencil. Using the questions on the page 12, try to record some of the versions of you.

The Last Bus, *26″ x 36″, recycled fabrics and sheep fleece on hessian. Designed and hooked by Diane Cox, Penzance, Cornwall, UK, 2012. "This is a memory from my teenage years in the north of England, where every winter it snowed. Saying goodnight to a boyfriend at a bus stop in the snow was a romantic experience!"*

"A man who trims himself to suit everybody will soon whittle himself away."

—Charles Schwab

Doris, My Nana, *18″ x 26″, recycled cottons and embroidery threads on vintage linen, with a painted brooch embellishment. Designed and hooked by Diane Cox, Penzance, Cornwall, 2017.*

"This is my Nana who did indeed work very hard all her life. I loved her very much. She was always singing, even though she had worries. She was an extremely gentle soul."

He Loves Me, *22" x 44", recycled cottons on hessian. Designed and hooked by Diane Cox, Penzance, Cornwall. "I made this rug to represent that very lovely moment when you realize someone loves you."*

Self-Reflection in Rug Hooking | 11

An Exercise in Self-Expression

Who have I been?

Think of past selves, all of our many abandoned personas: the track athlete, the dreamy schoolgirl, the café waitress, the nursing student, the young mom, the devoted employee, and so on.

_____

_____

_____

_____

Who have I wanted to be?

Your paths-not-taken are part of you. What career did you forego? Was there a time when life took a turn or took you away from something you wanted? Have you ever felt "there but for the grace of God go I"? What choices went unchosen?

_____

_____

_____

_____

Who am I now?

We are all much more than meets the eye. What is there about you that cannot be seen by a casual observer or even by those who know you well? Is there a hidden joy or sorrow? A private hope or ambition?

_____

_____

_____

_____

Who will I yet become?

We continually learn and grow. Some of us need to find our braver or more active self. Some of us need to be quieter and less hectic. What does your future hold, and who might you be in five years or in ten?

_____

_____

_____

_____

What is inside me, wanting to come out?

Think potential! Think courage! Imagine the someone you're longing to be.

_____

_____

_____

_____

_____

_____

_____

_____

_____

_____

Chaos, *25½" x 24½", #8- and 8.5-cut wool on linen.*
Designed and hooked by Sharon Townsend, Altoona, Iowa, 2010.

Variations on a Theme of Self-Reflection

In the planning of this book, we adopted one requirement: that the majority of rugs will depict the self in human form. Though we may identify with a creature, a landscape, a piece of art, or other non-human images, the thing that makes this book different from other rug-hooking books is the depiction of oneself in human form in nearly all the examples.

But because we inevitably come across exceptions that are, well, exceptional, let us include a few rugs here that resulted from self-reflection, but didn't involve the hooking of a human self.

Identifying with a Creature: Sharon Townsend

When Janice Lee traveled to Newton, Iowa, to teach her "Heirloom Rug" class to a group of Iowa rug-hooking friends, Sharon was among the students, even though her beloved husband had passed away only eight weeks earlier. Prior to the class, Sharon spent several days planning the design of a white rabbit on a crazy quilt background.

Sharon keeps a journal about the rugs she hooks, and she was kind enough to share her *Chaos* journal with me. The class roster and invitation, along with her teacher's business card and workshop photos, are tucked into the journal. She had taped many wool snippets inside her notebook to remind her what she had used in the rug. Contemporaneously, she wrote her thoughts each day about the process of hooking this rug, the friends who sat near her in the workshop, and where they dined each night. I have heard Sharon talk about this rug, and she describes the rabbit as "frozen" or "paralyzed." In the journal, though, there are no indications of Sharon's devastating loss, except for a single sentence near the end: "My rabbit is really me, sitting in the midst of chaos."

***Portrait**, 7" x 5", #6-cut wool on linen. Designed and hooked by Susan L. Feller, Augusta, West Virginia, 2014.*

Identifying with a Place: Susan L. Feller

I was chatting on the phone with Susan Feller about another self-portrait, when she mentioned this one. Although it depicts a place, she considers it a reflection of herself and how much she identifies with home. The close-up of the log cabin makes the colorful landscape even more vivid.

"The design was in response to Donna Hrkman's suggestion that I create a story for my self-portrait," Susan said. "The small format allowed for experimenting with colors and proportions. The blue-violet mountain range depicts an abstract value piece called *My Mountain State*. Trees are symbolic of my favorite subject (nature) and these shapes refer to the design *Mountain Treeline* by Anne-Renee Livingston, which I have hooked. We live in the log home we built. Eventually I will exhibit a collection of work depicting our log home, and this will be included."

Seampunk, 27½" x 20", #3-, 5-, 6-, and 8-cut wool on linen. Designed by Donna Hrkman and hooked by Luci Bolding, Omaha, Nebraska, 2016.

Identifying with a Story: Luci Bolding

Luci is a seamstress and a rug hooker, and the idea for this rug grew to encompass much more than her love of sewing. It tells a story of her values and her home state. A viewer might see Luci in the form of the courageous lion, driving her tractor/sewing machine on a creative adventure.

"My sewing machine rug was my take on Steampunk with Donna Hrkman," Luci said. "We used the sewing machine tractor; I do own the cast iron original machine the rug was drawn from. I used the lion from the Victorian era to show strength and courage. Since I was raised in Kansas and do love my memories there, we carried on with a *Wizard of Oz* theme. Hence the tornado, the fields, the sunflowers, the rainbow, and the lion. The red thread is a reference to Dorothy's red shoes. It was a very fun rug to make."

"A mind stretched to a new idea never resumes its original dimension."

—Oliver Wendell Holmes

Identifying with Shape and Color: Brigitte Webb

"Among other things, this rug reflects the trend these days for posting 'selfies' in the media," Brigitte said. "It's my tongue-in-cheek selfie. This abstract rug is also an attempt on my part to see myself in my rug hooking journey so far—my desire to learn, improve, meet new challenges, experiment, use different fibers—and to show various styles and techniques used in this wonderful art form.

"I also attempted to offer an insight into my personality, my willingness and enthusiasm to try different aspects of hooking such as abstract, geometric, and Waldoboro, to name but a few. I am happy to use any fiber that will hook up. This rug attempts to show how colorful and exciting it can be for those of us who wish to expand and grow. I gave this rug to a like-minded friend who is always challenging herself through her art."

See Me, *21" x 34", recycled wool, as-is and overdyed wool, sari silk ribbon, silk fabric, and velvet on linen. Designed and hooked by Brigitte Webb, Dingwall, Scotland, 2016.*

Identifying with Color: Lynn Goegan

Lynn adores color, identifies with color, and she uses every crayon in the box. She based this design on a piece of wallpaper from the 1970s. Often a mouse represents Lynn herself in her designs, and this little mouse is experiencing a virtual explosion of color.

Flower Power, *13" x 13", #4-cut wool and yarn on linen. Designed and hooked by Lynn Goegan, Sturgeon Falls, Ontario, 2017.*

Self-Reflection and Inspiration

Making a rug is a long process of sketching, pondering, designing, hooking, revising, viewing, finishing, and reflecting. As you read about and view the self-reflective works to come, I hope you'll keep your sketchbook handy and open your mind to inspiration and revelation. When you encounter that exciting spark of inspiration, let it flare up in your sketchbook or journal and fan it into a self-reflective rug design of your own.

A Time for Change, *21" x 30", #5-, 6-, and 8-cut and hand-torn wool and many other fibers on linen. Designed by Pris Buttler and Karen Greenfield and hooked by Karen Greenfield, Elkhorn, Nebraska, 2018.*

Karen hooked tulle, paisley, sheep's locks, sari silk, silk velvet, and synthetic fabrics into this rug, and she embellished it with vintage buttons and beads, belt buckles, and quillies. The Danish text in the rug is from Ecclesiastes: "For everything there is a season, and a time for every purpose under heaven." This verse has come to mean a lot to Karen.

"The woman in the upper part of the rug seems to be wearing a porcelain mask and performing for an audience. I used to be that woman who wanted to conform and do what was expected of her. But in the lower part of this rug, I have created another self, who is making up her mind who she wants to be."

18 | Rug Hooking Journeys

CHAPTER II

IN HONOR OF WOMEN:
DIANE COX
PENZANCE, CORNWALL, ENGLAND

Years ago, I discovered a group of rugs online. In the use of color, the choice of fabric, the subject matter, the sensibility they conveyed, these pieces were different from everything else I had seen. I studied and admired those rugs. I took screenshots and printed the images. As I look back now, I believe that what drew me to the work was how it communicated the identity of the maker. That was my first encounter with the art of Diane Cox, and in a big way, her work was the seed that grew into this book.

Here, you will have the unique pleasure of getting to know Diane for yourself. For me, her art is defined by three fundamental qualities: Diane's commitment to reusing discarded textiles and to preserving the handwork of other women; her lifelong love affair with making art; and her passion for honoring women—their stories, their work, their joys, and their suffering—in her designs.

There are elements of art that we can explain and illustrate, and there are other elements that come through to the viewer in subtler ways. For me, Diane's work is endowed with conscience, camaraderie, and liberation. From her choice of fiber to her choice of subject, she tries to do what is right—keeping old textiles out of the landfill—and show what is true, by shedding light on untold stories of women, yesterday and today. Often, she reaches out to other women, connecting with them through her art. In a single piece, she might depict a chapter of women's history and incorporate a special piece of tapestry or embroidery or part of an old quilt she has saved, so that other women, other makers, are present in her rugs. And finally, Diane follows her own bliss and creates her own versions of beauty, which cheerfully disregard many conventions and rules.

***Self-Portrait**, 12″ x 12″, recycled fabric and dyed wool on hessian. Designed and hooked by Diane Cox, Penzance, Cornwall, UK, 2008. "I worked from a photograph, under the excellent teaching of Jean Schroderus," Diane said.*

Girl from the North Country, *26″ x 34″, recycled cotton and wool, sheep's fleece, assorted fabrics and old blankets, and embroidery thread. Designed and hooked by Diane Cox, Penzance, Cornwall, UK, 2017.*

"This one is to represent all those wonderful evenings as a teenager," Diane said, "when I would escape from the house and have fun with my friends. I am from the north originally, and the winters were really cold. So I often put snow and rain into my rugs. As girls, we didn't care about the weather!"

In Honor of Women | 21

Scarlet Woman, *18" x 22", recycled fabrics, tiny Suffolk puffs, embroidery, and an original "Ban the Bomb" button on hessian. Designed and hooked by Diane Cox, Penzance, Cornwall, UK, 2017.*

"I hooked this to show how older women can get out there and really enjoy life," Diane said. "They can demonstrate about causes close to their hearts, be free, make their mark. Although I wouldn't usually have a red coat on a pink background, I just really wanted to. It is meant to be a snowy background but full of joy!"

22 | Rug Hooking Journeys

Reading Woman, *30" x 54", recycled wool, cotton, sheep's fleece, vintage linens, embroidery threads, and tapestry piece (the cat). Designed and hooked by Diane Cox, Penzance, Cornwall, UK, 2016.*

"I love reading," Diane said, "and Persephone books are wonderful with their beautiful dove grey covers and endpapers of textiles related to the period in which the novels are set. I found the tapestry cat in a charity shop and knew that one day I would put him into a rug. At the moment, Reading Woman *is hanging in my kitchen and is a calming influence.*

In Honor of Women | 23

An Interview with the Artist

Author Tamara L. Pavich: We rug hookers all have collections of wool, but your beautiful studio is filled with textiles of all kinds, blankets and quilts and fabrics that you've gathered and collected. Please tell us about your love of textiles.

Diane: Growing up, I was surrounded by textiles. All the females around me were sewers and knitters. "Waste not, want not" was still a maxim adhered to in Yorkshire in the 1950s, so garments were taken apart and made into something else. The women made coats for the children, or they made one dress from two worn dresses. That's how it was in those days. And then the fabric not suitable for clothes was chopped up and put into rugs.

I learned all these skills at a very early age, although I never made a rug back then. I watched my mother and grandmothers make them. Stone floors were cold, and hooked and prodded rugs were warm to the feet. It always seemed to me that making rugs was a soothing occupation, a time when women could chat and not have to think too much.

TLP: So hooked rugs were part of your childhood, even though you didn't hook back then?

Diane: The rugs in my grandmother's farmhouse were huge, heavy, and dark. Regularly, we would drag them outside to be beaten with a carpet beater. Occasionally we cleaned them by hauling them around the field in the morning dew—great fun for children. Canadian rugs are often cleaned by being put outside in the snow, but this wouldn't work in Britain because the snow is too wet and slushy.

TLP: What led you to hooking rugs yourself?

Diane: Hooking came later on. Art was my main subject when I trained to be a primary school teacher, and teaching young children is a highly creative process. I spent my school holidays indulging my desperate desire to stitch, usually clothes or curtains.

It really wasn't until I had a serious illness and took early retirement from teaching that I had time to develop my love of textiles in a more artistic way.

It was my good fortune to meet a 91-year-old lady in a care home who had hooked rugs all her life. Sadly, she wasn't allowed to have her rug-hooking equipment in her tiny room, but she was determined to use her fingers to create. She made flowers out of yarn and stitched them on to small pieces of backing to make lap rugs. She was delighted to meet someone interested in making rugs, and she gave me her extremely well worn and much loved hook, which I treasure. That was over twenty years ago.

. . . .

The Simple Pleasures, *18" x 21", recycled fabrics, cottons, sari silk, embroidery thread, and tapestry piece on hessian. Designed and hooked by Diane Cox, Penzance, Cornwall, UK, 2017. Diane hooked this rug to express the feelings of someone recuperating from a serious illness, content to enjoy those little moments of pleasure that perhaps in ordinary life she would not appreciate so much. "When I started the rug," Diane said, "I had no idea that this idea would emerge. I wanted to use part of an old tapestry to hook a lady with a bird in her lap. As I was hooking, the meaning became obvious to me."*

In Honor of Women | 25

TLP: When you began, what were your desires for your rug making endeavors?

Diane: I had no plan other than to make my house beautiful and always to use recycled fabrics, as had been done traditionally. My children were older, and I was determined to fill the house with homemade rugs. Using my children's outgrown clothes would also enable me to hook memories into my rugs.

As the floors gradually disappeared beneath the rugs, though, I began to put them on the walls too. Now, there are rugs everywhere: floors, walls, the backs of chairs and sofas, on beds and window seats. Aging rugs have their own beauty, and I love it when they look faded and worn. I move them around as was done in times gone by, the last port of call being the outside loo and the shed!

TLP: At some point, rug hooking became a more reflective or self-reflective process for you.

Diane: Yes, and it seemed to happen without my realizing it. I love stories and narrative and found that my rugs were telling little tales, probably stories no one would know except me. I found it exciting. Researching the female line in my family tree, I learned that many of the women had worked in the cotton mills in Lancashire, and several had lived and worked amongst the woolen mills in Yorkshire. One had been a silk spinner. They all had had quite hard lives. This made me want to tell their stories and also to tell some of my own.

In general, women's lives over the centuries fascinate me. All my figures are women, because so many in the past did not have voices. Their lives were deemed of lesser importance than men's lives, and so their stories were not recorded.

Wash on Monday, 29″ x 18″, *recycled fabric hooked on hessian, with hand-embroidered linen apron. Designed and hooked by Diane Cox, Penzance, Cornwall, 2012.*

"This lady was part of a women's history project in Penzance," Diane said, "in conjunction with the Hypatia Trust. It was called the History 51 project because 51 percent of the Cornish population are women, but in all the history books a woman is rarely to be seen. This project was intended to redress the balance and to raise awareness of some unsung Cornish women. Our hooking group created a template of a woman so that we could hang the women to look as if they were all holding hands. I chose to represent my Cornish husband's female ancestors, all wives of fishermen, all working class, some of whom lost their children to the great migration to America and Canada for mining. I portrayed a careworn woman; I embroidered various names of Mike's ancestors on the dress, and on the apron, a poem about working.

"We all decided to have our ladies wearing aprons to unify them. We used all recycled fabrics and lots of vintage bits and bobs for the embellishments. It was a wonderful experience, but sadly the funding ran out and it had to end. However, we give our hooked ladies an outing every now and then, and they will be exhibited at the new Hypatia Trust in Penzance this summer. The Hypatia Trust has a huge library of literature by and about Cornish women."

Sewing in Front of the Rayburn, *30″ x 36″, recycled cottons, sheep's fleece, Lurex, wools, two small pieces of vintage fabric, and embroidery thread on hessian. Designed and hooked by Diane Cox, Penzance, Cornwall, 2017.*

"I love my Rayburn," Diane said. (For American readers, this is a warm stove.) "I love lighting it. It is solid fuel and very cozy, great for cooking in the winter. This rug shows one of my biggest pleasures in life."

Admiring the Rug, *38" x 33", a mix of recycled fabrics with sheep's fleece, wool yarn, and old blankets on hessian. Designed and hooked by Diane Cox, Penzance, Cornwall, 2013.*

"This rug really is a slice of life," Diane said, "a frequent occurrence amongst rug hookers. The small, ordinary, domestic parts of life are very important to me: having a chat with friends; sharing a pot of tea; eating homemade cake; getting excited about color, fabrics, and design; being cozy indoors when it's grey and gloomy outside.

I make at least one proddy mat each winter. They keep you warm whilst you are prodding. I wanted to mix proddy with hooking in this piece, so in this picture, I like to think I am showing off my latest winter proddy mat to my friend."

Many years ago, one of my aunties wrote and illustrated two books just for the family. Each chapter told a story of her childhood, her grandmother's, and her great-grandmother's. Her books were hugely inspiring to me, and I am doing something similar with my rugs now, telling untold stories, capturing moments of women's lives, including my own, which can be passed down through the generations. It is so satisfying to hook a rug with meaning, such a sense of completion. In fact, it's an absolute necessity now to have story and meaning.

TLP: You are a member of a very creative group of rug hookers. I wonder whether you prefer the inspiration of the group or the solitude of creating by yourself.

Diane: I love the bonds that form amongst people who have grown to know each other well, initially through the shared joy of rug hooking. Women still use sitting with handwork in a group as a safe place to solve problems and put the world to rights, to laugh and to cry. Working with women who have suffered domestic violence really opened my eyes to the benefits of making rugs in a safe, calm environment. So the support of a group, the encouragement and constructive criticism, and the inspiration of seeing everyone's work all make the group experience special. Living in the far west of Cornwall, I am surrounded by a community of artists and can dip in and out of workshops and courses, all of which contribute in some way to my work.

However, if I need to concentrate, particularly when hooking a face or developing a new idea, then I need to hook alone, listening to music or BBC Radio with a pot of tea close by and usually a dog at my feet.

TLP: Can you describe the place that art occupies in your life?

Diane: My mother sketched and painted, and I was always drawing as a child. I allow myself time to study art books and to visit exhibitions, installations, and galleries. Art makes me think, feel, smile, ponder, and even if I don't like what I'm seeing, it can be a stimulus for conversation or ideas.

More specifically, I am drawn to the human face and figure, particularly female, time and time again. Colour is all. I can sit and look at a certain combination of colours and feel happy. It could be a green jug of daffodils on a pink table, just simple things that nurture and soothe.

TLP: Would you say your hooking space is messy or tidy?

Diane: My studio is usually gloriously messy—full of fabric, books, and art materials. I can't work in a tidy way because I am "painting" with fabric, and you can't mix colours as you can with paint. I have to have all the colours spread out around me. I need a huge quantity and large variety of fabrics. If I tidy up, which I have to do occasionally, it becomes difficult to find what I want!

My studio constantly draws me: the smell of the hessian, the coziness, the light. In the studio, there's a sofa, two worktables, a coffee table, a day bed, and lots of old painted wicker chairs covered in cushions and throws. And of course, the odd rug! There are fairy lights and candles, a tea urn, teapots and cups, a radio and CD player. Behind the studio is a field of horses. In front I look down on the rooftop of our cottage and, farther, to the sea. I feel very lucky to have such a big and wonderfully light space at the top of the garden. I could quite happily live in there.

TLP: Do you hook every day or do you keep to a schedule?

Diane: I do tend to work steadily most of the time, and if I go away, I will take some stitching with me. It's more portable than hooking, especially on a train. Most of my rugs now incorporate an element of stitch, which has gradually evolved through a love of hand-sewing and the desire to experiment with adding texture and other elements to my work. The stitched parts of my rugs can take a long time to do, but I love the slowness and the actual process of the needle pulling the thread through the backing.

Making rugs is an integral and normal part of everyday life. I stitch or hook or cut strips or draw or make a collage every day. If I don't, I feel bereft! Even a few minutes a day adds up. I always have several rugs on the go at any given time, so I can choose which to work on, depending on my mood.

TLP: You hook with so many different fibers. What are your favorites?

Diane: Textures excite me, so I love to mix materials. I use tweedy woolens with delicate silks and worn cottons, plus knitting yarn, lace, Lurex, and sheep's fleece.

My choice of fabrics is pretty much anything and everything, as long as each one has had some sort of previous life. A shocking amount of fabric and unwanted garments still go to landfill each year, which horrifies me. A garment in a charity shop made from the most horrible synthetic fabric in jazzy colours can often become amazing in a rug. Many a time, I've slipped quietly out of a charity shop hoping no one will see what I have bought!

I love the way patterned fabric can hook up in the most surprising and unusual ways, and how a printed fabric that doesn't look right can add to the effect if you hook up the unprinted side. Just a touch of glitter or lace can give your design a lift.

I have always been of a mind to "Make do and mend" or "Waste not, want not." I love that a rug can never be replicated, because it all depends on what recycled fabrics you have at any one time. That's the beauty of it.

TLP: As a student of your work, I have noticed themes of domesticity, honoring hard-working women, thrift, romantic love, family love, and happiness with oneself and one's life. While many of your rugs highlight the positive aspects of being a woman, there are glimpses of some difficulties in the experience of being a woman, too.

Diane: I have never really analyzed it before, and this question has really made me think about these ideas quite deeply. I agree with your summary of the themes in my work. I think I could see from an early age, having been told little girls should be seen and not heard, that women were the peacemakers. Their strength was quiet, not loud and shouty like my father. But I couldn't work out why women also seemed submissive. I also hugely preferred the company of women. As I grew older, it made me angry that it seemed to be a man's world still. I went into teaching because at that time it was the only job which had equal pay regardless of gender.

From early childhood, my confidence was actually eroded by my father. But I have gained confidence from my thirties onwards until I am now, at sixty-six, more confident than I ever was. Having survived cancer at thirty-nine changed me and set the path that I have been following ever since.

Bag Lady, *16" x 24", all recycled fabrics plus a piece of tapestry on hessian. Designed and hooked by Diane Cox, Penzance, Cornwall, UK, 2017.*

"At one point in my life," Diane said, "I used to carry all my important documents in my handbag wherever I went. It was after my divorce, and I didn't feel safe leaving them anywhere. This rug depicts that time."

Waiting, *25" x 26", recycled fabrics plus vintage fabrics with embroidery on them for the appliquéd pots of flowers on hessian. Designed and hooked by Diane Cox, Penzance, Cornwall, UK, 2016.*

"This rug shows a woman who could be from any era," Diane said. "She is waiting for something. In so many situations in life, women have to wait, and I wanted to portray that in this rug. It doesn't really matter who or what she is waiting for. People can imagine for themselves. I had been reading books about the Second World War and thinking about all those women who got on with life at home whilst waiting for news of their husbands, fathers, and sons away at war."

That period was also when I first started to hook rugs, and eventually I wanted to express myself more. That's when my "lady rugs" began. I don't plan them too much and I never think about what others may feel when they see them, because I am just expressing something within, something personal. I just HAVE to hook them. It's a compulsion.

It is always lovely, though, when a rug of mine touches someone in some way. I recently sold my pink "Ban the Bomb" lady (*Scarlet Woman*) and was interested to know why the purchaser had chosen that particular rug. She said she had seen the strength of an older, confident woman in it.

TLP: Will you please say a bit more about the Waiting rug and the Secrets rug and any of these rugs in which you have touched on how a woman's life can be difficult precisely because she is a woman?

Diane: *Waiting* was inspired by women in World War II, waiting for news from their loved ones. As this woman emerged, I realized she could be from any time in history. Women do indeed wait. My grandmother had four sons away at war, and I often wonder how she coped with the waiting. My other grandmother had two children out of five with epilepsy and an older, frail husband to care for. She cleaned people's houses and must often have been waiting for some respite, some rest. I have this rug next to my bed and look at it every night. It calms me.

As a child I was told, "Little girls should be seen and not heard," so I became a very good listener. Everything I have stitched into the *Keeper of Secrets* rug is a real secret that I heard spoken by the females in my family when they thought I was reading or playing. I love reading the words and like to imagine my grandchildren reading them too and learning about their ancestors' stories. This rug reminds me that throughout the centuries there have always been problems, troubles, scandal, secrets.

The Keeper of Secrets, *28" x 65", recycled fabrics plus part of a vintage chintz quilt. Designed and hooked by Diane Cox, Penzance, Cornwall, UK, 2017.*

"The coat is made from my mother's favorite mohair winter coat from the 1970s," Diane said, "difficult to hook and a labor of love. The dress is part of a large piece of patchwork from the 1920s to 30s era, which still had the paper and card templates inside it. The templates were parts of letters and legal documents and I wanted to keep them. So I stitched through those, another labor of love!"

TLP: You mentioned having taught rug hooking to women who had experienced domestic abuse. What was it like for them to make rugs?

Diane: Several years ago I was asked to teach a group of ladies at the local Women's Aid unit. These women had spent time in the refuge, having experienced domestic violence, and were now ready to go out more into the world and to rebuild their lives. None of them had ever seen a hook, and many were adamant they were not creative or arty.

This time was one of the most rewarding and satisfying experiences of my life—to see how they gained in self-belief, self-esteem, and self-confidence as the months went by, not just in their ability to hook, but in all aspects of their lives. Most had very little money, and so the recycling of old garments was a perfect thing for them to do. What was said within the confines of the group was sacrosanct.

One might have hooked a rug depicting the view of a garden of a house where she felt safe, a rug to place beside the bed, little pictures of pets. The rugs they made were full of life and colour, often intended for children and grandchildren, but also for themselves. Sometimes a woman would arrive and perhaps just sit quietly, not feeling like hooking that particular day. That was okay.

The more they hooked, the more confident they became. The work of some of them was unique and stunning. Some women were amazed that they had produced such artistic work, and this encouraged them to continue, to look at artists' work, to visit galleries and grow.

A short animated film was actually produced about what the hooking group had done for the members. The film started quite darkly with actors speaking the words (for the safety of the women), describing their terrible experiences. But the film became lighter and lighter with humour and love and finished with a picture of a child flying away on a magic carpet, hooked, of course. In the film, the ladies talked about what the group meant to them: something to look forward to each week, somewhere they could forget everyday worries, a precious few hours when they could devote themselves to doing exactly what they wanted.

The group still exists. There are new members all the time, and the strength of the group remains.

Detail from The Keeper of Secrets.

Contemplation, 23" x 23", *a mix of hand-cut recycled fabrics, cottons, acrylics, and wool, on hessian. Designed and hooked by Diane Cox, Penzance, Cornwall, 2013.*

"This rug came out of a group challenge," Diane said. "I collect things—broken pottery pieces with writing and beautiful designs, tiny pot lids, glass stoppers and marbles, old buttons, parts of delicate ornaments—that I find in the fields where I walk my dogs. All very inspiring!"

Diane put these items into grab bags to be chosen by members of her group. "My bag contained several pieces of an old clay pipe," Diane said, "which immediately brought to mind a picture of an old Romany woman reflecting on her life whilst enjoying her pipe. My drawing was very simple, and as I was hooking her, I felt my way into her personality. She gradually emerged, and the piece of old Victorian silk quilt was perfect for her shawl." (Diane used embroidery on a piece of a Victorian silk quilt, hand-sewn on top of the hooking.)

34 | Rug Hooking Journeys

The Day the Buzzard Came, *36" x 26", recycled fabrics, sheep's fleece, and a small embroidered piece on a vintage bit of quilt. Designed and hooked by Diane Cox, Penzance, Cornwall, UK, 2016.*

"This is the story of the day my dad died," Diane said. "The sentence 'The owls were restless' refers to the owls on my bedroom roof the night before he died. I heard them and couldn't believe the noise, and my neighbour said he could see them. There were quite a few! I do believe owls can portend events, and the next day I heard my father had passed away. I had to hang out my washing in the garden, and as I did so, there was a dreadful noise in the sky, quite unearthly. I looked up to see a buzzard circling overhead. I have heard buzzards many times, but this was a most extraordinary sound. He circled closer and closer until he was right overhead. I knew it was my father. He loved birds and was also not the easiest of characters, and so it made absolute sense to me that he was saying goodbye to me in buzzard form. This is a very personal piece."

"It's an absolute necessity now to have story and meaning in your rug."

TLP: Some of your rugs seem to encourage women to see their own beauty.

Diane: Beauty does come from within. As many women my age do, I look at photos of myself as a young woman and think I was lovely. But at the time, I really did think I was hideous. So some of my rugs do offer that encouragement. I love the wisdom of older women. Being older and more confident, having experienced much, we can feel more beautiful than when we were young and plagued with self-doubt. I love expressions on faces, not frozen, rigid, perfect masks. I love faces that show the lives they have lived.

> "I love expressions on faces, not frozen, rigid, perfect masks. I love faces that show the lives they have lived."

Hippy Chick, 15" x 20", recycled fabrics. Designed and hooked by Diane Cox, Penzance, Cornwall, UK, 2017.

"She represents my student years in the early seventies," Diane said. "Our hooking group decided to hook faces to represent ourselves, but it wasn't necessary that the faces look like ourselves. The young hippy chick took me by surprise as I hooked, because I thought I would be hooking an older woman. However, *Hippy Chick* appeared and that was that."

CHAPTER III

MYTH AND FOLKLORE:
ANN WILLEY
COMSTOCK PARK, MICHIGAN

An Interview with the Artist

TLP: *You are clearly a prolific painter, Ann, but how did you get started with rug hooking?*

Ann: My story as a rug hooker really begins with my story as an artist. My mom and dad met in art school, so I grew up in a family that valued the arts. I ended up studying art in college with a concentration in printmaking. After my college years, I worked in graphic design and illustration, and when I raised my children, I began to search for a medium I could use in the home—one that would fit into fractured days.

I began to understand the appeal of textile work that could be picked up and put down as needed and could travel fairly well. At that time, my mother was dabbling in rug hooking and had purchased a large stash of wool and equipment from an older rug hooker who had become too arthritic to hook. My mom took some classes and created some lovely things, but ultimately decided it was not for her, so she offered the supplies to me.

TLP: *How lucky for you!*

Ann: Yes, and I was smitten by the sight of all that lovely dyed wool. Working with color was a big part of my art, and the woolen colors were so beautiful. I recalled how I loved going to yarn stores with my mom as a child and seeing all those lovely hues tucked on shelf after shelf.

TLP: *Did you take any rug hooking classes?*

Ann: I just dived in. Hooked rugs reminded me of woodcuts, and I pulled out my books of prints and scoured them for inspiration. Also, I had always loved folk art and folk patterns. Vintage rugs in the primitive style inspired me. And hunting for wool and dyeing the wool was fun, too.

TLP: *So what is the relationship between your painting and your rug hooking?*

Ann: My main goal was to translate my simpler, more graphic painting style to hooking. A gallery began showing my hookings alongside my paintings, so I have always looked upon them as fine art, just another medium for self-expression which my art making had become.

I would begin a hooking with a simple sketch. Then a session at the dye pot to get a sense of the colors I wanted to work with. I found the process of rug hooking to be fluid and spontaneous, because the image would change as the work progressed.

For many years, I made small wall hangings. The supply of wool I had been given by my mom was in strips cut to #4, and despite experimenting with other cuts, that became my preferred size to work with. I had always been drawn to creating more intimate, small-scale art. By keeping the finished pieces small, I could explore more ideas.

TLP: *I'm sure you've been told that your works look like little tapestries.*

Ann: I do love how a finished piece is contemporary, but it also resonates with past textile traditions.

In Her Element, *11" x 13", wool on linen. Designed and hooked by Ann Willey, Comstock Park, Michigan, 1998.*

TLP: *For me, there's a literary vibe too. Clearly, you're telling stories, but can you talk about how you incorporate folktales into your designs?*

Ann: A love for stories, myths, and poetry has informed my work over the years. Classic stories often communicate basic human struggles and emotions. When I let my imagination wander through these tales, I find motifs that resonate with my own experiences. In other words, the content of a larger story becomes personal for me. The stories that I remember for many years become entangled in my everyday life, and they become a source of imagery for my art.

TLP: Can you articulate how this is helpful and useful to you?

Ann: Well, it enables me to see my life in a broader perspective, and to see that my life parallels the experience of others. Rug art becomes my means of processing and sorting through life's experience, separating the wheat from the chaff, and finding the treasure.

TLP: That must be very rewarding.

Ann: Yes. But the challenge is that my work is personal and original, and I am putting it out there. So it can feel kind of risky to share it with the world. Now that I'm older, I am more comfortable with that. People either get it or they don't. And it feels great when I hear comments that someone really enjoys the work and it speaks to them on a personal level. It is very affirming to find that an image is meaningful to others. When art works, it touches something in others that they recognize.

TLP: Does rug hooking ground you or soothe you? Is it a release?

Ann: Rug hooking has two personalities. On the one hand, when the day is stressful and I can't focus on much of anything, I can always pick up my rug hooking. It becomes a kind of meditation. I can listen to music or turn on *Law and Order* reruns, and just let my mind catch up with my body. I can think about my day as my fingers work, and I can just appreciate the tactile quality of the wool and the lovely colors. Yes, it is grounding and soothing.

The other side of rug hooking requires focus, decision making, struggle. Is the imagery working? Are the colors harmonious? Am I capturing the right emotion? Difficult choices must be made, and strips of wool are pulled out and replaced.

TLP: Is that avoidable? Or do you think we just have to do it over sometimes?

Ann: I try making paper cutouts and setting them on the linen to work out issues of scale or patterning. Still, sometimes I must sacrifice a lovely stretch of hooking because it doesn't work anymore with the image as a whole. Very often I have to return to the dye pot to get the shades of color I need.

I have learned to let the work sit out of sight for a while, so I can see it with fresh eyes before I begin to pull things out and make drastic changes. Other helpful techniques are photographing the work and checking it in gray values, or flipping the work to see its mirror image. This can reveal an area that isn't working.

TLP: Some artists thrive on community, while others work alone. What about you?

Ann: Hooking for me is either a quiet task where I can rest my mind, or it is a focused task where I am engaged with working out the imagery. Either way it is difficult to have others around. I especially love the meditative moments of working. I am pretty far along on the introvert scale, so I need solitude to recharge and relax.

Also, usually people are shocked when I am basically ripping things out to make changes. So that part of creating I do alone. Sometimes I find myself stuck, and then I do show a piece to a few trusted friends and ask for feedback. That can be very useful.

TLP: Some artists work steadily all the time. Others have dormant periods and bursts of productivity. What is your pattern?

Ann: I think artistic slumps happen to all artists. I am away from my creative work quite often, and when that happens, I just have to take the time to find my way back. I try to trust the process and not get too frustrated when nothing seems to be working. It's like feeling around in a dark room. You know your stuff is in there. You just have to find it.

I find it's helpful to sketch a little before bed, with no judgment or plans: playing in the studio, being bold, forcing myself to jump in the deep end. I actually think I make an extraordinary amount of work that is just not that great, but you have to push through and keep searching.

TLP: The distinct look of your rugs is partly due to your use of color. Where do you find your wool?

Ann: I work with recycled and new wool. In thrift shops, I am always on the lookout for an unusual color. Then I often make stews where I marry different colors together very quickly. I used to dye all my own blues, but they seem to turn gray over time, so now I overdye an off-the-bolt light blue. And I use coffee a lot to age and soften colors.

Lately I have been using found woolen clothing to bleed out some dye and throwing lots of others colors into the dye pot. These have to be closely watched. I have sometimes ended up with a kind of muddy earth color, but that can be useful too. My handling of colors has changed a lot over the years. I used very strong colors in my earlier pieces, but now I am trying to create more subtle color shifts.

TLP: Do you have a studio in your home? Where do you hook?

Ann: My rug-hooking domain has moved around over the years. I have a studio now, and I store my wool in drawers and bins sorted by color. However, I have found painting and rug hooking in the same locale don't mix. If I work in the studio, snippets of wool begin to spread across my painting surfaces, and I get wool fibers showing up in my paint strokes.

So I usually hook in a comfortable chair with music and TV nearby. I am pretty messy, and while I am busily hooking, the wool begins to pile up around me on tables and spills out of baskets at my feet. I have little sketches nearby, and color references. It can get pretty out of control. My cat is usually taking a nap in one of the baskets. He loves it when I rug hook. My husband, not so much.

TLP: For you, what are the rewards of making art?

Ann: In general, art in my life seems to be about processing and finding solace, and exploring a spiritual and psychological landscape. The ceramist Harvey Sadow wrote: "Art opens doors, shines light into darkness, speaks about things left unsaid . . . . Art reminds us of grace."

Setting Out, 10½″ x 13″, #4-cut wool on linen. Designed and hooked by Ann Willey, Comstock Park, Michigan, 2004.

"The image sprung from my fascination with the Persephone/Demeter story of Greek mythology," Ann said. "Demeter's daughter Persephone is taken to the underworld by Hades. Persephone leaves her mother's home, taking the promise of warmth and flowers with her, and moves alone into a shadowy world. Demeter grieves her loss and allows the world to become barren while she is gone.

"Setting Out *is about that pivotal moment in so many stories, when the heroine takes up her destiny and ventures into the unknown. This resonated in my life at the time. My youngest child was leaving the nest and taking off into the big, bad world on her own. She struggled, but like Persephone, emerged intact and whole.*"

Myth and Folklore | 43

The Yellow Bird, *11" x 14½", #4-cut wool on linen. Designed and hooked by Ann Willey, Comstock Park, Michigan, 2011.*

"My figures are not always related in a linear way to a specific story," Ann said. "It is more apt to say that they are composites of many characters and a bit of myself. This could be Rhiannon, the Queen of the Fairies, with a songbird, which were sacred to her.

"I find myself making images of women holding plants and flowers a lot. I have recently read that this image is very ancient and still can be seen in folk textiles like embroidery. In ancient times the figure was a nature goddess associated with fertility."

Common Ground, *13" x 18½", #4-cut wool on linen.*
Designed and hooked by Ann Willey, Comstock Park, Michigan, 2016.

"Growing up, I loved spending time with D'Aulaires' Book of Norse Myths," *Ann said. "We had a beautiful copy in our home. Frigg was the goddess of beauty, love, and family. One of the stories that stuck with me was the tale of Frigg and her son Balder. After dreaming that her son would die, Frigg set out to obtain a promise from all living creatures that they would not harm her son. She overlooks the mistletoe, which is then fashioned into an arrowhead by her enemy and used to kill her son. I guess it spoke to me of how difficult it can be to protect our loved ones from harm."*

Myth and Folklore | 45

The Art of Infusing Rug Designs with Folklore

Featured artist Ann Willey has made a study of ancient myth and folklore, and this knowledge has informed her beautiful designs. How can those of us who haven't devoted ourselves to the study of mythology learn from Ann Willey and infuse our work with lore and legend?

Start with a Scene or Image

"Sometimes there is an image in a story that just sticks with me," Ann said, "and I can't really say why. If I find myself working with it in my art, the significance can sometimes work its way to the surface. Sometimes I think they are just delightful images that are enjoyable to play with." Is there a scene from a fairy tale that captures your imagination?

Place Your Heroine in the Scene

To tell a tale, we need a heroine. Place your heroine in natural surroundings, as Ann has shown us, perhaps dark and foreboding, or maybe with a distant horizon behind her. Your heroine may be escaping or departing from a house or place. Her facial expression may be reflective, pensive, cautious, or determined.

Endow the Design with Imagery

Lavish attention on the nature imagery, rendering leaves, branches, plants and flowers in beautiful detail. Forest creatures (Ann often employs birds) may accompany your heroine on her journey. The heroine may be wearing magic clothing, always visually interesting, patterned, and beautiful. Common patterns in borders and clothing are vines, florals, and repeating shapes.

The Importance of Nature

"I have a lot of references to nature in my work," Ann said, "especially birds and plants. I find myself making images of a woman holding plants and flowers a lot. I have recently read that this image is very ancient and still can be seen in folk textiles like embroidery. In ancient times the figure was a nature goddess associated with fertility." For examples, see *The Night Garden* and *The Yellow Bird*.

Dress for Journey, 11" x 17", #4-cut wool on linen. Designed and hooked by Ann Willey, Comstock Park, Michigan, 1995.

"My favorite tales usually involve a hero or heroine undertaking a dangerous journey," Ann said, "a sort of quest. In 'East of the Sun, West of the Moon,' the young daughter must travel to the ends of the world to find her beloved. The heroine must go through many challenges: separation from her family, navigating through a strange and lonely world, and at the conclusion, a return to wholeness. The magical dress represents the transformation she will undergo."

Inferring Meaning in Your Tale

"Another way to look at a fairy tale," Ann said, "is that all the characters represent aspects of yourself. Seen in this way the woman character or heroine becomes a representation of the process of becoming one's true self."

> "When I let my imagination wander through these tales, I find motifs that resonate with my own experiences."

Change of Seasons, *11" x 13", #4-cut wool on linen. Designed and hooked by Ann Willey, Comstock Park, Michigan, 2003.*

"Three of my rugs, including Change of Seasons, *were hooked when I was exploring the classic myth of Persephone and Demeter and how it was playing out in my life. My youngest child, my daughter, was leaving home, and I was experiencing a 'change of seasons.' Watching our children move out into the world and make their own way can be difficult for any parent. My daughter did find her own path, but spent some time in a 'dark woods.'"*

Vista, *11" x 13", #4-cut wool on linen. Designed and hooked by Ann Willey, Comstock Park, Michigan, 2005.*

"This little hooking captures that gaze that turns inward," Ann said. *"The word 'vista,' meaning a distant view, is here referring to looking inside as well. She is the heroine from a story, remembering a journey she has made, or reflecting on a challenge that she has faced. And now it is evening, and it is time to rest."*

Between Earth and Sky, *18" x 12", #4-cut wool on linen. Designed and hooked by Ann Willey, Comstock, Michigan, 2013.*

"This hooking is a little tribute to the marvelous intelligence that is an owl," Ann said. "Every spring our woods are visited by owls, and they appear at random through the summer months as well. To have an encounter with such a creature brings you to pause and hang in the moment. Everything else falls away, and you are gifted with a glimpse into another world."

"It's like feeling around in a dark room. You know your stuff is in there, you just have to find it."

Ocean Window, 12" x 15", #4-cut wool on linen. Designed and hooked by Ann Willey, Comstock, Michigan, 1996.

"I don't recall the tale that first introduced me to the idea of underwater cities where people live," Ann said. "There are a few stories that I have since found, one of a kingdom that was flooded by a magical fountain while the king and his family were feasting and despite being underwater they are dancing, and eating, and partying still. For some reason the notion of people living ordinary lives at the bottom of the sea has always intrigued me."

Myth and Folklore | 49

Morning Light, *13″ x 18″, #4-cut wool on linen. Designed and hooked by Ann Willey, Comstock Park, Michigan, 2015.*

"In a garden, two women sit as the morning light surrounds them with its warmth," Ann said. "In my mind, the two are close friends or sisters: two sides of a coin, a duality, but not opposites. A thread of friendship and familiarity wraps around them, and they are mirrors for each other, an echo, a call and a response. One of my sisters is a year older than I, so we grew up together, and that relationship is a confirmation of who we are."

"Art opens doors, shines light into darkness, speaks about things left unsaid . . ."

—Harvey Sadow

The Selkie, *11" x 17", #4-cut wool on linen.*
Designed and hooked by Ann Willey, Comstock Park, Michigan, 2017.

"This is a folktale that I have explored a lot in my paintings," Ann said, "and it seems like time to do another version in rug hooking. The story of the selkie is another Celtic tale, also called 'The Seal Wife.' A selkie is a shape-shifting creature that can live both on land and in the sea. On land they appear human, but in the sea they take the form of the seal. The selkie in the tale has her seal skin stolen by a fisherman, whom she marries and with whom she raises a family. One of her children discovers her seal skin, and she returns to the sea. There is a lot of Scottish lore about selkies moving and even living among the villagers, appearing in long, black coats. Sometimes they bring luck, other times, if they are mistreated, they bring troubles."

Where She Dwells, *13½" x 16", #4-cut wool on linen. Designed and hooked by Ann Willey, Comstock Park, Michigan, 2012.*

"A love for stories, myths, and poetry has informed my work over the years. Classic stories often communicate basic human struggles and emotions."

The Night Garden, *9" x 11", #4-cut wool on linen. Designed and hooked by Ann Willey, Comstock Park, Michigan, 2011.*

"*The Night Garden depicts a place where transformation, discovery, even danger can occur,*" Ann said. "*Here might be a passage to another world that lurks beneath or beside our own. Fruits and flowers stolen from the enchanted garden propel the heroine into an unintended place. In the fairy tale, 'The Handless Maiden,' the heroine sneaks into the king's garden at night to steal pears and is discovered.*"

Myth and Folklore | 53

Bird in Hand, *13½" x 17", #4-cut wool on line. Designed and hooked by Ann Willey, Comstock, Michigan, 2009.*

A portrait of Ann's daughter, who like several other girl characters, is accompanied by a colorful bird. A possible reference to the proverb, "A bird in the hand is worth two in the bush," piques the viewer's interest as well.

Portrait of a Boy, *11" x 14", #4-cut wool on linen. Designed and hooked by Ann Willey, Comstock, Michigan, 2003.*

This is a portrait of Ann's son, to which she hoped to give "a storybook feel." Upon studying the boy's face, it's surprising how little shading was done to achieve this likeness. The strong presence of the extra-wide borders of colorful geometric shapes gives these portraits added significance.

"Art in my life seems to be about processing and finding solace."

CHAPTER IV

SYMBOLS AND THE SELF:
HÅKON GRØN HENSVOLD
SKREIA, NORWAY

For many years, Håkon Grøn Hensvold, a teacher of textile arts in his village, Skreia, Norway, near Oslo, has created tapestries, weavings, and quilts. It wasn't until 1998 that he made a trip to the Vesterheim Norwegian-American Museum in Decorah, Iowa, where he first saw hooked rugs. Although he was teaching other textile arts, he was drawn to the class on rug hooking, and before he left for home, he had taken a lesson and purchased the equipment and materials to carry with him back to Norway.

We are very fortunate indeed to feature an artist who is also a teacher, a Norwegian who is bilingual and who is articulate in English, and a magical storyteller who fills his designs with symbols and meaning.

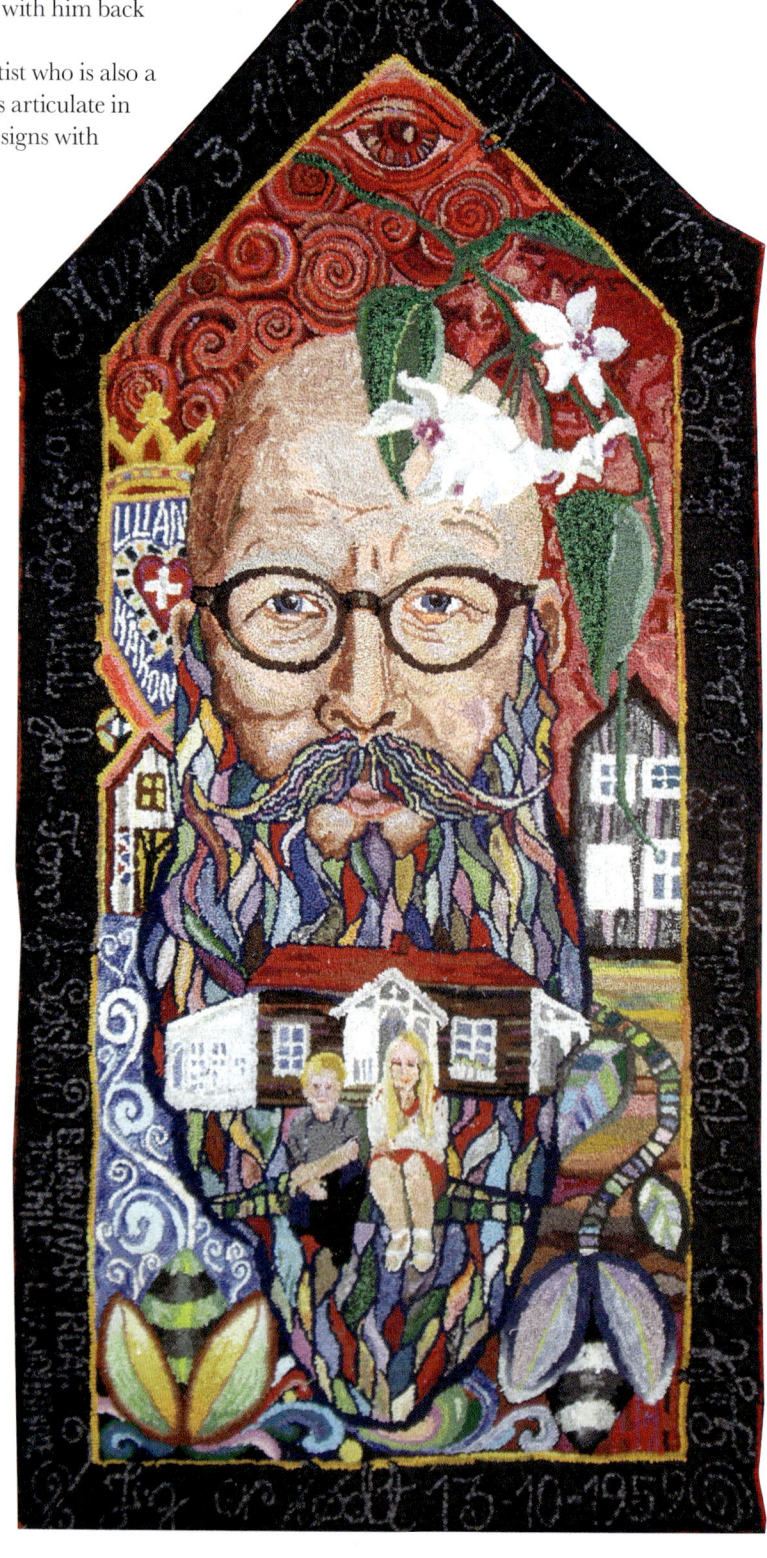

Self Portrait, *114 cm x 170 cm (roughly 45" x 67"), #5-cut wool on linen. Designed and hooked by Håkon Grøn Hensvold, Skreia, Norway, 2011.*

"Creating a self-portrait is a challenge," Håkon said, "because it reflects yourself. Those who look at it when it's finished should see who you are and what you stand for. It is difficult.

"I wanted to put things that are important to me into my design. My children and our house are in the center of my beard. My wife's name, Lilian, is in the heart at the left. I collect hoya, a houseplant. I have about 150 different hoya, so I had to put in one such flower. The border is my memo pad for old dates: my birthday, my wedding, my children's birthdays, and the names of my mother and father and my siblings.

"The rest of the symbols are a little harder to tell you about. It is my own symbolic language that I create and that you will find in my other work. A house. The flower. The eye, and others. I want these symbols to be open to interpretation and leave the viewer to make their own opinion. Why do I have a colored beard? It's about to be gray in real life. I think it's my way to show the colors that are inside me."

56 | Rug Hooking Journeys

I Wish I Could Fly, *65 cm x 136 cm (roughly 25.5″ x 53.5″), #5-cut wool on linen. Designed and hooked by Håkon Grøn Hensvold, Skreia, Norway, 2016.*

"The angel with the sunflower just appeared in my sketchbook one autumn," Håkon said. "It stayed there to the spring and then he became a design for a rug. I have often thought that if I didn't know that winter comes between autumn and spring, the logic would be spring comes after autumn, new life after death. The text around the border goes like this: I wish I could fly like an angel over village and town and sprinkle the autumn sun above and beyond everybody who needs to awake again."

Symbols and the Self | 57

An Interview with the Artist

TLP: We have entitled your chapter "Symbols and the Self," so we'll be talking about your use of symbols. But first, have you always been a storyteller?

Håkon: I started to express myself in pictures as a teenager. As a young boy sitting in his room, drawing and listening to music, I started to notice that everything fantastic could happen on paper. In the beginning, it was difficult to put meaning into figures and to build up stories. Probably, I had not lived enough yet. After a while, though, I developed, and the pictures began to have some meaning. It became easier when I went to school and learned more. I was fond of modern art, and some artists meant a lot to me. Through looking at these artists, I understood the importance of creating a signature way to draw.

Last night I found my old drawings from that time, and it was really interesting to see them again. Some of the pictures had the beginning of stories that are in my rugs today. To tell a story is a long process.

TLP: Can you describe how you go about telling stories in your rugs?

Håkon: To make stories is a bit like a mosaic. You have to put one piece with the next one, and together they make meaning. First, you must have an idea of what you want to make a story about.

For an example, we can look at the rug called *Sisters*. I have two sisters, and the idea was to try to tell a story about them, or any two sisters. I started with the faces and the hair. The hair binds them together, and this is the first symbol. Their bodies become the shape of a cocoon or a jar—symbol number two. They have one arm each and they hold a bird and a flower—more symbols. The bird is oriented upward, and the flower is oriented downward. This gives a symbolic meaning, but it's important also for the composition of the picture. The upward and downward directions are helping to make movement. I framed the sisters in the shape of a house, a symbol of their parents' home. On either side of the women, there are two more house shapes, one pointing up and one pointing down, and the directions are opposite from the bird and the flower. This tells something about each sister. The houses in the back are a symbol of the village or the rest of the world, and the tree is a symbol of time, family, roots, and growth. There is a person in the village. Who could that be?

TLP: It must be you.

Sisters (Line Drawing), *114 cm x 170 cm (roughly 45" x 67").*

Sisters, *65 cm x 120 cm (roughly 25½" x 47¼"), #5-cut wool on linen. Designed and hooked by Håkon Grøn Hensvold, Skreia, Norway, 2014.*

"To tell the story about sisters isn't easy," Håkon said. "I have tried to show the difference between them and at the same time the similarity. They are connected by family but separated by choice of life. The blue bird flying out contrasts with the lily's heavy smell of presence. They both look at us and ask the question: Is this the quilt of life?"

Håkon: Now, the next thing is to bring color into the drawing. It matters whether the bird is white or blue, and if the flower is red or yellow or white. If you change all the colors, the design will totally change meaning. This rug would have a different meaning if the main color were blue instead of ocher and earth colors.

When I make a rug, I always have in mind that the design shall offer more than one way to interpret it. I believe there is always more than one way to see the world. My way is okay, but it's also interesting to hear how others see. It makes me reflect and to go on with my thinking. When people tell me their interpretation of a rug, I know that they have used their eyes and their minds. I know that I have started something, evoked a reaction in them. That is more important than my story, but I'm always pleased if they see my meaning too.

TLP: Many rug hookers deliberate about the words "craft" and "art" to describe rug hooking. What do you think about these words?

Håkon: I like to say that we would not have art if we didn't have craft. I think craft is the skill you need to make art. If you are using craft to reproduce another's design, then you are a craftsman. When you are able to use the craft to express your own meanings, thoughts, feelings and so on, then you are an artist.

When you feel comfortable with a technique, you stop worrying about how to do it and start thinking about what to use it for. You have some choices. You can make rugs for decoration, use patterns from others, or you can make your own patterns. The rugs are craft and they function as that. They give the makers great joy during the making and after, when they are used. When I see other rug hookers' work I am often impressed with their technique and their skills.

I didn't call myself an artist before I had my first exhibition. I think you have to show your work and have an audience first. This is a complex subject, but I am glad there are groups out there who are working in this craft and that there are artists among them.

TLP: What artists have influenced you? What is it about their works that you may have emulated?

Håkon: There are many, both international and Norwegian artists. Some Norwegian artists are Gerhard Munthe, Edvard Munch, Kai Fjell, and Terje Ythjall. International artists include Gustav Klimt, Vincent van Gogh, Marc Chagall, and Friedensreich Hundertwasser.

If you look at these artists, most of them are very fond of colors, and so am I. I have always loved color since the first set of markers I got as a kid, bright and clear colors. As an adult, I have learned that you need the dull colors, too. If you don't use them, the bright colors will just kill each other.

I play with colors in every rug and discover new combinations every day. I don't have any worms left over in my box, because I blend them in and get a new color combination, and that gives me a thrill. But my heart belongs to bright colors and intense expression.

TLP: Please tell us how you learned about rug hooking and how it became one of your favorite textile arts.

Håkon: My first exposure to rug hooking was in Decorah, Iowa. In 1998, I had been invited to teach weaving and felting at the Vesterheim Norwegian-American Museum, the most comprehensive museum in the United States dedicated to a single immigrant group. In between my classes, I looked at works from the other classes that were being held that summer. In one room, there were two ladies demonstrating rug hooking. I am a curious person and asked them to show me how this rug hooking was done. They said I would be able to learn it in fifteen minutes. That was true, because it was all the teaching I ever received.

My first reaction to this new craft was that it looked just too simple. Why didn't every loop just pull out? My second reaction to rug hooking was that this was a wonderful way to make patterns in all directions and switch colors as often as you pleased. It seemed to be much faster than tapestry or weaving. Before I left for home, I was able to buy a book, a hook, and a cutter. It was two years before I actually tried to work on my first rug.

My first mat (page 76), was brightly colored and had a pattern I had designed. Designing my own rugs was one thing that fascinated me about this new technique I was learning.

To my surprise, it was as easy as the ladies told me, and I really enjoyed rug hooking. I saw that the technique was suitable for my way of making pictures.

TLP: What was it about rug hooking that won you over and caused you to become so prolific?

Håkon: I am a person who likes to work with textiles; they appeal to me through their softness and variety. After my first rug, I started to make rugs that tell stories. The technique suited me, because it allows you to work freely, and there are almost no rules you have to follow. I had tried tapestries, but I found it too slow and too complicated for me to express myself, and there were many rules. Rug hooking has many of the same qualities as tapestry, but it's easier to work with.

Norway has a rich tradition in weaving and tapestry, and I like to look at that history to find my own identity. After my first rug, I understood that I had to learn some things before I could express myself in the technique. So I worked slowly to make a few large rugs. In recent years, I have worked faster. I feel I have found the right medium for telling my stories.

The Singer, 112 cm x 80 cm (roughly 44" x 31½"), #5-cut wool on linen. Designed and hooked by Håkon Grøn Hensvold, Skreia, Norway, 2013.

"The Singer is a portrait of my son Eitif," Håkon said. "He is a talented man, who at the time I made this rug, went to school and was taking a class in singing and songwriting. I try to express the wonder a good performance and a good song can create, from the butterflies in the stomach to the stars in the night."

Symbols and the Self | 61

Dandelion, 115 cm x 82 cm (roughly 45¼" x 32"), #5-cut wool on linen. Designed and hooked by Håkon Grøn Hensvold, Skreia, Norway, 2016.

"This is the story of the troubled children I meet in school where I work," Håkon said. "They may have different problems to deal with, and they need different kinds of help from different kinds of people. Like dandelions, they struggle through school and still shine like small suns. They sit in class, and scribbling in their notebooks is all they achieve. You can see the scribbles are the border around the rug. This is the first rug of three with this theme I have made so far, and I hope there will be many more with stories from my experiences in school."

62 | Rug Hooking Journeys

1 + 1 =, 45 cm x 64 cm (roughly 17¾″ x 25¼″), #5-cut wool on rug warp. Designed and hooked by Håkon Grøn Hensvold, Skreia, Norway, 2017.

"This is a portrait of a pupil from school who often behaves differently than the other pupils," Håkon said. "He never knows why he does the things we don't want him to do. His heart is dark, and the bird is his flight out. The border shows the scribbling he makes instead of homework, and the emojis are his reward. But still, he wears his hair as high as a crown."

Symbols and the Self | 63

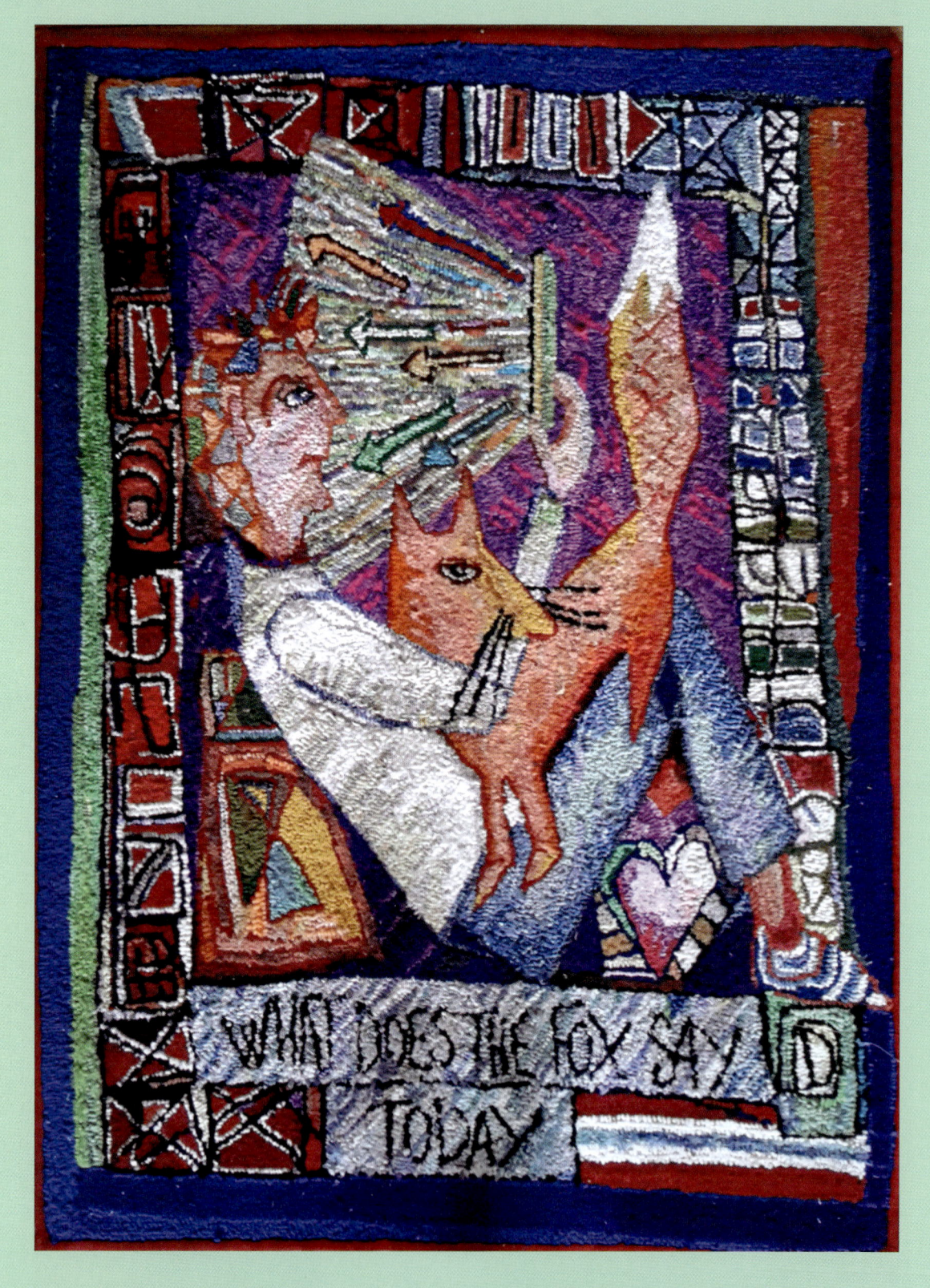

What Does the Fox Say Today?, 68 cm x 93 cm (roughly 26¾" x 36½"), #5-cut wool on rug warp. Designed and hooked by Håkon Grøn Hensvold, Skreia, Norway, 2017.

"Young people are using their mobile phones for everything," Håkon said, "and they disappear into their phones. In school, I often see that they believe everything they find on the Internet. The fox is my symbol that they have been tricked out of the truth and out of their time. The border is scribbling on the wall, which I have used to connect this rug to the others in the series, Dandelion and 1 + 1 =.

Bendik og Årolilja, 94 cm x 110 cm (roughly 37″ x 43″), #5-cut wool on linen. Designed and hooked by Håkon Grøn Hensvold, Skreia, Norway, 2002.

"This is my interpretation of a famous old Norwegian folk song, 'Bendik og Årolilja,'" Håkon said. "The story goes like this: Bendik falls in love with Årolilja, the daughter of the king. A little boy tells the king that Bendik visits his daughter, and the king condemns Bendik to death. Årolilja prays for him, without success. Årolilja dies of sadness, and they are buried on either side of the church. Up from the two tombs, the lilac grows up and over the church roof. I have put the words from the refrain in the rug, and it says: 'Bendik went to see the maiden, that is why he had to die. Årolilja, why do you sleep so long?'"

Symbols and the Self | 65

TLP: Now it seems that rug hooking is a big part of your life.

Håkon: To make art is important to me, and textile arts work with my personality. It takes some time and allows me to rejoice in the material and the process. To make art is a way to work with the things I encounter in my life. When I work on one rug, I am thinking about the next one. It's a good thing that it takes some time, so that I can plan a new rug. It is also a driving force for me. The older I become, the more important it is for me to make good art. I feel a great joy when people interpret my rugs and find their own stories. Then I think I achieved something.

In April of 2016, I had my first exhibition. It was very special to see all the rugs I had made on the walls. For the first time, I could see the connection between them, and I could hear them speak. Maybe at the moment when the last rug was up on the wall, I understood that this is something worth sharing. The exhibition helped me see myself as an artist and not just as one who makes craft for craft's sake.

TLP: Are you part of a group in Norway, or do you pretty much practice alone?

Håkon: For the most part, I work alone. I never discuss my subject matter with anybody. It's important for me to develop it my way. In Norway, there are not many rug hookers. I have started a little group that meets every month. They are working on their rugs, and I am like a mentor for them. They are usually the first ones to see my rugs, and they tell me their thoughts.

But to work alone gives me a freedom which is important for my creativity. As I said earlier, I need time to develop my stories.

See Me, 80 cm x 114 cm (roughly 31½″ x 45″), #5-cut wool on linen. Designed and hooked by Håkon Grøn Hensvold, Skreia, Norway, 2010.

"Youth are always in need of being noticed," Håkon said. "The girl is asking the mirror, the boy is expressing himself by acting out. In the back are houses, one for each season. Time will go by, and the story will repeat again and again."

Three Women in the Village, *106 cm x 150 cm (roughly 41¾" x 59"), #5-cut wool on linen. Designed and hooked by Håkon Grøn Hensvold, Skreia, Norway, 2012.*

"I have played with the words 'three' and 'tree'," Håkon said. "In Norwegian they are spelled similarly. So, the story can be about the tree in the village, about the three women in the village, or about both. The border is filled with birds, flowers, and hearts, so it's likely to be telling something about love. The yellow cat and the raven represent the wisdom and free spirit."

Symbols and the Self | 67

TLP: Do you work in a home studio?

Håkon: Believe it or not, I work in our living room in front of the TV. That is where I hook. I do have a workroom on the second floor, where I keep all my wool. It is roughly sorted by color in plastic boxes.

I have a wife who is understanding and allows me to have my work in the living room. This is natural for me, because rug hooking is something I do in my free time, and I still want to be part of our family life. In the corner of my living room, I have a basket with the wool for the rug and my cutting machine. I use a box with small compartments to keep the worms in, so that when I start on a new rug, I'm organized. After a while, it is chaos in that box.

TLP: Where do you find wool to use in your hooking, and do you dye your own wool?

Håkon: I use some recycled wool, but mostly I use new wool fabric. It is not too hard to get in Norway, because it is used in our folk costumes and clothes. I like to dye. I use Remazol dye, and sometimes I dye with plants. I haven't mixed other fabric or fibers into my rugs, except when I need gold (color). Then I allow myself to use synthetic material.

> "I have learned that you need the dull colors, too. If you don't use them, the bright colors will just kill each other."

> "Rug hooking has become more and more important... I feel I have found my medium to tell my stories in."

TLP: Do you have any suggestions for rug hookers who want to use symbols in their rugs?

Håkon: I think of the heart—a symbol known to us all. The heart can change form, size, color, and direction in the picture. It could be precise, or elongated, or widened. It doesn't have to be a perfect shape, but the suggestion of the symbol means love to most people. Depending on how you distort it, or where you place it, or what color you might hook it, this symbol could mean something unique in a rug. And this is true of other symbols too.

TLP: Do you work every day or most days?

Håkon: In the beginning when I started with rug hooking, I worked now and then. I could take long breaks while working on a rug. I have other crafts that I do, and sometimes they would get all my attention.

The weekends and holidays are prime hooking time for me. I like to make big rugs, so they take some time to finish. I start a new rug only when I have finished the last one. I can't work on two at the same time. I'm a teacher in arts and crafts during the school year, so that takes a lot of my time.

The last four years I have worked more and more with rug hooking and less of the other crafts. My sketchbook is full of ideas, waiting to come alive.

Håkon's workstation: *I tape the drawing of the rug to the lid of a box so I can control my choices as I hook. When I am finished hooking for the day, I always hang the rug on the front of an old cupboard in the living room. Every time I sit in my chair, I look at the rug in progress. This gives me some perspective, so I can find out if things are working as I planned.*

Symbols and the Self | 69

The Rooster Is Dead, *256 cm x 90 cm (roughly 101" x 35½"), #5-cut wool on linen. Designed and hooked by Håkon Grøn Hensvold, Skreia, Norway, 2009.*

"This is a complicated rug to explain," Håkon said. "I hope there are many stories in this rug, and that it can be told in many different ways. The centerpiece is a rooster hanging from a cross. This motif gives the rug its German title: der Hahn ist tot, which means 'the rooster is dead.' This is a children's song we sing in school when we start to learn German. It goes like this: 'The rooster is dead and it cannot sing anymore, koko koko koko kokodi, kokoda.'

"The dead rooster is a contrast to all the other things that happen in the rug, celebrations of love and life. But I'm not sure if the mouse agrees."

70 | Rug Hooking Journeys

"At the moment when my last rug was up on the wall at the exhibition, I understood that this is something worth sharing."

It's a Suitor in the Garden, *71 cm x 101 cm (roughly 28" x 39¾"), #5-cut wool on linen.*
Designed and hooked by Håkon Grøn Hensvold, Skreia, Norway, 2013.

"I'm so lucky to have a daughter whom I love," Håkon said. "When she was young, I promised her that the day she started to bring home suitors, I would stand on the porch with the rifle and send the suitors away if I didn't like them. That didn't happen at all. She found the best husband, and now I have two grandchildren. I had to make a rug about this, and you can see me with the white cat at the right and the son-in-law on the left, reaching his hand up and saying 'I will.' My daughter is on the porch, smiling, and is pleased with it all. This was my wedding gift to them."

The Virgin Rug, *112 cm x 144 cm (roughly 44″ x 56¾″), #5-cut wool on linen.*
Designed and hooked by Håkon Grøn Hensvold, Skreia, Norway, 2016.

"*The Virgin Rug is my free interpretation of the story of the good and the foolish virgins from the Bible,*" Håkon said. "*It is a well-known design that was widely used in tapestry in Norway in the sixteenth and seventeenth centuries. The design is based on the parable about the ten virgins who were awaiting the arrival of the bridegroom. Half of the virgins were prepared and had with them extra oil for the lamps they carried, in case his arrival was delayed. The other virgins had brought only their lamps. As we might expect, the bridegroom's arrival was announced after midnight. The wait had been long enough that the virgins who did not have extra oil had to leave to find more oil for their lamps. While they were gone, the bridegroom arrived and, greeted by five virgins with brightly glowing lamps, took them away to the marriage feast. Who are the good virgins and who are the bad? That depends on the viewer who is looking at the rug.*"

The Journey, *81 cm x 118 cm (roughly 32″ x 46¾″), #5-cut wool on linen.*
Designed and hooked by Håkon Grøn Hensvold, Skreia, Norway, 2014.

"We all have to travel sometimes," Håkon said, "and take a journey where we don't know the destination."

74 | Rug Hooking Journeys

Huldresølvet, 102 cm x 144 cm (roughly 40″ x 56¾″), #5-cut wool on linen.
Designed and hooked by Håkon Grøn Hensvold, Skreia, Norway, 2015.

"A hulder is a seductive forest creature found in Scandinavian folklore," Håkon said. "The rug is about a girl who looked after the cows in the mountains in summer. She was in love with the youngest boy on a big farm, but he had an older brother who would inherit the farm. She struggled to decide who she would choose; love or wealth.

"She got a visit from the huldre-people and they gave her some traditional jewelry and told her to say yes to the first man who asked to marry her. They planned that it would be the huldre-king who asked first, but the older brother was quicker. And the girl had to say yes as she promised. The youngest brother was then desperate so he asked the huldre-people for help. They took the older brother inside the mountain, and he became a huldre-person too. Now the girl has the boy and the farm and the silver, and they should live happily ever after. But the huldre-king casts a spell on the farm, and all those who use his huldre-silver.

"This is a story that lives in the dark woods in Norway and has been an inspiration for many art forms. I have made the story with the girl who keeps a traditional drinking bowl, where you can see the house on the farm and two dark figures, who are the two brothers. The girl is whirled into a dance with the huldre-people that you can see dancing in the border around the rug."

My First Rug, *81 cm x 58 cm (roughly 32" x 23"), #5-cut wool on linen. Designed and hooked by Håkon Grøn Hensold, Skreia, Norway, 2001.*

"The design is my signature flower," Håkon said. "I had not collected much wool yet, so I had to use what I had. I had bought some Kool-Aid to try dyeing with (Kool-Aid is not available in Norway). That rescued the design from only dark and dull colors. This rug has lain on my floor since I made it, and the dog and the cat like it. It is my test of how strong rug hooking is and how long it will last with daily use."

76 | Rug Hooking Journeys

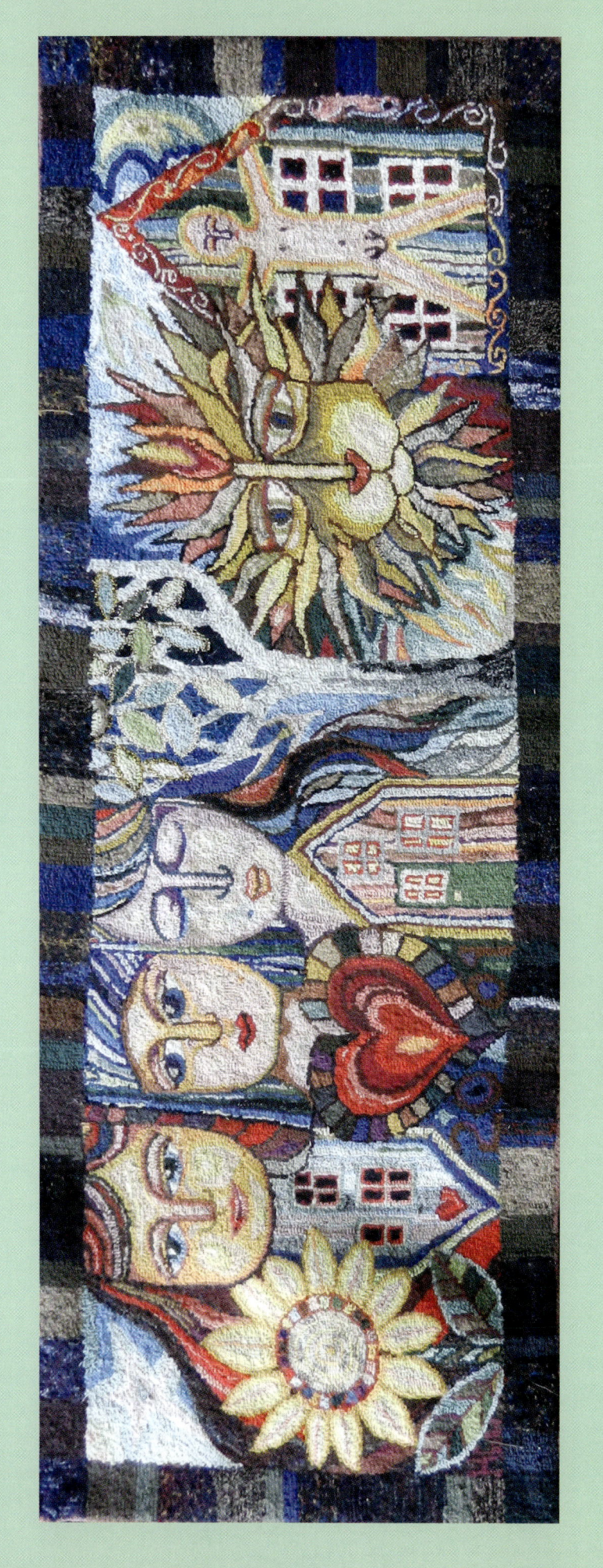

Bedrunner, 151 cm x 56 cm (roughly 59½" x 22"), #5-cut wool on linen. Designed and hooked by Håkon Grøn Hensvold, Skreia, Norway, 2001.

"This is the second rug I made," Håkon said. "For me, it shows the joy of rug hooking and all the possibilities. It gave me a thrill to make it. The three girls in different moods just came along. The tree in the middle separates the girls from the lion and the naked man in the house. This is a bed runner and every morning, I put my feet down on the faces of the girls and they never complain. But sometimes I can hear the lion roar."

Symbols and the Self | 77

No One Can Understand that Only This Little . . ., *90 cm x 142 cm (roughly 35½" x 56"), #5-cut wool on linen. Designed and hooked by Håkon Grøn Hensvold, Skreia, Norway, 2005.*

"This is a story about love, given and taken," Håkon said, "about happy love and unhappy love. The border has a text I will try to translate:

> To dream a dream in every day's hiss
> are the seas waves in the inner ear
> punch by punch against the rolling stone
> grinded without edges, round slippery, cold
> wake up and say 'I will' and be free."

78 | Rug Hooking Journeys

The Seed, *64 cm x 91 cm (roughly 25¼″ x 36″), #5-cut wool on rug warp. Designed and hooked by Håkon Grøn Hensvold, Skreia, Norway, 2017.*

"When things happen in life, it is inspiration for a new design," Håkon said. "When I was told I would be a granddad again, I made this design, the woman holding the seed that is going to be the new life and all the heart power she is going to use from the start to the end. She is like the tree with branches stretching out, always loving and caring."

Symbols and the Self | 79

CHAPTER V

PAST, PRESENT, AND FUTURE SELVES

If we pare down the idea of a self-portrait, the very basic idea is to answer this little question: How do I look? The idea is broadened considerably, though, by the rug hookers represented in this chapter, who have asked and answered other questions in their works. How do I see myself? Might I capture something more than my appearance, like my character or identity, in this image I am hooking? Who was I in the past, and who might I become in the future?

Along with successful, present-tense self-portraits from Brigitte Webb, Sharon Townsend, Susan Feller, Laura Pierce, and Val Flannigan, we include rugs that carry us forward or backward in the life of the rug hooker: Donna Hrkman looks back on herself in the arms of her doting mother; Marilyn Becker reflects on her rural Wisconsin childhood; Trish Johnson remembers college days; and Holly McMillan looks forward to wearing purple spectacles when she is older.

We have also collected rugs that offer a different kind of glimpse into the identity and mind of the rug maker. While Val Flannigan dreams of travel, Janet Conner shows us the world represented in her DNA. Lilly Phillips exaggerates an everyday moment in her backyard, while Cathy Stephan identifies with a classic work of art. Both Karen Greenfield and I attempted to hook a state of contentment in the present moment.

Feeding the Forest, 37″ x 28″, #7- and 8-cut wool on linen. Designed by BJ Colwell and Lilly Phillips and hooked by Lilly Phillips, Council Bluffs, Iowa, 2017.

When I started working on this manuscript, my mom, Lilly, and I talked about hooking funny moments in our lives and how we might condense them into one frame, a single rug. She decided to exaggerate a moment in her life. While she loves to put out feed for the wildlife in her woodsy backyard, she has been astonished that her home has become a favorite eatery for whole herds of deer. She has seen as many as 20 at a time, and some will not run when she comes out to refill her feeder. So, in the spirit of the tall tale, she hooked her little self with her little bucket of corn and hungry deer as far as the eye can see. She thanks her longtime friend, BJ, for the help with the drawing.

Smile, Please, 20″ x 24″, #3- to 6-cut dyed wool, as-is wool, and recycled wool on linen. Adapted from a friend's photograph, designed, and hooked by Brigitte Webb, Dingwall, Scotland, 2017.

"This is another first for me," Brigitte said. "I had not attempted a realistic self-portrait before. I chose a photo that a lifelong friend took, one of the few that I like. It is a reflection of how others see me, and indeed, how I see myself—someone who smiles a lot with a humorous twinkle in the eyes.

"Having not attended any classes on hooking faces, and only consulting my wonderful books, I sought advice from a great friend who hooks magnificent faces. I asked her to draw the design for me, but she encouraged me to try. I am so glad I did. Thank you, Dana. She also gave me pointers on hooking skin tones and hair, for which I am so grateful. One of the very best things for me in rug hooking is having supportive and encouraging friends who are willing to share their knowledge and abilities.

"I changed many aspects of this portrait several times—the eyes, skin tones, and hair—until I was happy with it. Getting the smile right was the hardest part of this rug for me, but, thankfully, I remembered this advice: When hooking teeth, hook the loops horizontally, so that each loop shows a natural gap, which is what I did. I honestly still find it hard to believe I actually created this piece of work. Thanks, Tamara, so much for the opportunity of doing so for this book."

Uncharted Waters, *32" x 38", various cuts of wool on linen. Designed and hooked by Sharon Townsend, Altoona, Iowa, 2004.*

    Sharon hooked this rug in Burma Cassidy's class on self-portraits. The technique that Burma taught was to hook on a blank canvas, working from a large copy of a photograph, putting in the lines and shapes from the photo, and gradually building the portrait. "I started with the black part of my nose," Sharon said. "I measured it on the picture and then hooked that shape without drawing on the linen. I was sitting next to Patty Yoder, and I kept saying out loud, 'This is very hard.' Patty would say, 'You can do this, Sharon.' I only drew shapes or dots on linen while I worked, but there was no picture drawn when I started.

    "My kids tell me that this expression on my face was one they remember very well from their childhoods. They would have liked a smile better."

    Sharon also noted that she is very grateful to Jim Lilly for making this custom frame.

Past, Present, and Future Selves | 83

No Greater Love, 22½" x 30", #3-cut wool on primitive bleached linen.
Designed and hooked by Donna Hrkman, Dayton Ohio, 2017.

"My younger brother found a cache of old slides my father had taken and decided to convert them to a DVD for my mother. We found one of my mother holding me when I was about six months old. I'd never seen it before. I was overwhelmed by the photo: the amount of love showing in my mother's face is immeasurable. I knew it would be a rug the moment I saw it.

"It's a self-portrait in the most abstract sense; I'm too young to even talk! But the self-reflection comes from the clear expression of love radiating between my mother and me, and how I knew growing up that she and my father loved me right from the start. I remember my happy childhood and Mom's ongoing help and support through my life. She's still proud of who I've become, and I'm grateful for her always being on my side. I know that bond will remain between us always."

This monochromatic rug was hooked with ten values.

Good Old Holly, *19" x 24", #3- to 5-cut wool on linen.*
Designed by Donna Hrkman and hooked by Holly McMillan, Roca, Nebraska, 2018.

"When first approached about this project, I was so excited," Holly said. "What would I do? How would I want to portray myself? Should I be young, or old? Should I do my alter ego? Could I be a superhero? Ultimately I decided on an elderly Holly. Since nobody knows how I am going to look when I am older, I felt a sense of artistic license.

"I usually wear tortoise-shell glasses, which are pretty neutral, but I hope that when I retire and no longer have to dress for others, I can wear purple glasses and funky clothes. It was so much fun when my teacher read me the poem 'Warning: When I am an old woman, I shall wear purple' by Jenny Joseph. I had never heard it before, but it was perfect for my project.

"I attempted to age and shape myself into the woman I will be in the future, surrounded with the words that created the person in the rug: family, love, faith, and compassion. I purposely faded out the background into black to represent the fact I too will fade into the distance someday. I hooked 'MD,' as I am a physician of internal medicine and spend most of my time taking care of the elderly. As most of my patients will say, 'You're only as old as you think you are,'—and I plan to be young forever. I plan to go out of this world with a smile on my face and a twinkle in my eye.

"Note that I am still wearing my hooking apron, so no need to guess what I am doing when I am older."

Past, Present, and Future Selves | 85

Where I Belong, *25" x 24", #6- and 8-cut wool, wool yarn, and dyed seam binding on linen. Designed and hooked by Tamara Pavich, Council Bluffs, Iowa, 2018.*

"For ten years I was an expatriate of a sort, having been transplanted from my Iowa home to Hawaii. Of course, I wanted to be with my new husband, who is part Hawaiian. I loved the beautiful climate and took great interest in the convergence of many cultures in Honolulu. But no matter how long I lived there, I was a perpetual outsider, a *haole*, even among people I knew rather well. I missed being known and understood. (Other *haoles* did understand.) I longed for the sight of a cornfield, the caw of a crow, and the familiar prairie landscape. When we moved back to Iowa in 2008, I remember boarding the plane with such a sense of relief, a feeling that I didn't have to try so hard anymore, but I could be understood as myself again. I was coming home, where I fit into my surroundings."

Namaste, *18" x 18", #6- and 8-cut wool, sari silk, synthetic fabric, yarn, a felted sweater, and dyed seam binding on linen, designed and hooked by Tamara Pavich, Council Bluffs, Iowa, 2018.*

This is a version of my character, Bea, in Namaskar pose. I kept her features very simple—her face is literally a few lines—so that I could be mindful of the meaning of Namaste while I hooked. To quote Isabelle Marsh, "Namaste is a thank you to the world. It says that the divine in me honors the divine in you." Her eyes are downcast or closed because she is attuned to what is inside her more so than to outside influences. It has been a pleasure to hook this serene round-faced woman a few times. Maybe she's my Buddha. There are more versions of her in Chapter VII. I think of her as someone I could emulate. She's helping me to find inner peace.

Portrait of the Artist, 27" x 26.6", #4-cut wool on linen. Designed and hooked by Trish Johnson, Toronto, Ontario, 2018.

"This is an adaptation from my own sketch, which I found in a sketchbook from August 1976. I looked back at this sketch to a time when I had the leisure to study my reflection in a teakettle and draw it. But many busy years have come and gone since then, and now I am finally at a stage when I have the leisure again to actually adapt my drawing into a hooked piece."

88 | Rug Hooking Journeys

Susan @ 60, *12" x 16", #6- and other cuts on linen along with wool appliqué, cotton threads, sea glass necklace, and a linen shirt. Designed, hooked, and worked by Susan L. Feller, Augusta, West Virginia, 2014.*

"I took a workshop with Donna Hrkman," Susan said, "to begin this portrait. From a photo I took, she enlarged and sketched the face. I also went through the same process to familiarize myself with the lines and separate me from the subject. Throughout the entire creating time, I found myself critiquing how I thought I looked rather than the reality. The lips were taken out three times, and I still think there is something off in that area.

"The best advice from Donna was that my background was another space to tell my story. Instead of using the curtain material I had been standing in front of, there are elements of my artistic and personal life. We live in a log home, the blue/purple mountains refer to an award-winning piece *My Mountain State*, and the trees are recognizable subjects in my work. They are an homage to the design and *Celebration* selection *Mountain Treeline*."

Laura at Cambria, *10" x 13", #4- to 8-cut wool on linen.*
Designed and hooked by Laura W. Pierce, Petaluma, California, 2008.

"Having spotted a couple of wide-cut scrap portraits online by Patti Stephens and Nancy Terhaar in Oregon, I wanted to try my hand at it, too," Laura said. "Using a photograph by Lloyd Heinze from Cambria Pines Rug Camp, I created a pattern for a self-portrait. But could I make it look like me? Soon, I felt like my brother was looking back at me. Yay! A family resemblance! I hooked day and night for a few days, caught up in mindfulness of values and dimensions. The bits of unexpected color from the noodle bag give liveliness to the portrait. The background and shirt were done with spot-dyed wool from my stash, and the burgundy collar was from the scrap bag. While ignoring most suggestions, I did keep adding a bit more smile until my friend, Peggy Northrop, was happy. I'm very grateful for her insistence."

This rug was juried into the 2009 Sebastopol Center for the Arts *Portrait* show and included in *Hooked Rug Portraits* by Anne-Marie Littenberg.

Realistic Self Portrait, 5″ x 7″, #3-, 4-, and 5-cut wool on linen.
Designed and hooked by Val Flannigan, Kelowna, British Columbia, 2011.

"I had signed up to take a class with Laura Webber Pierce on hooking portraits," Val said. "I had never hooked a portrait before and was not sure of my ability to capture the essence of someone. So as not to offend anyone by not making it really look like them, I chose to hook a self-portrait. I found that the mauve was very useful in capturing the shadows and coloring of an older person."

Past, Present, and Future Selves | 91

***Magellan's Ship**, 60" x 48", hand-cut wool on linen.*
Designed and hooked by Janet Conner, Hiram, Maine, 2017.

"I did genome testing to learn my genetic make-up," Janet said. "Then I collected pictures of the ancient boat designs from the various ethnic groups, and finally I realized that all the lands the Portuguese explorers found and colonized are exactly where my DNA comes from. Even the 4 percent Native American is probably from Brazil (colonized by Portugal), as genetically we do not distinguish between North and South America.

"So, I have the ship of the famous Portuguese explorer, Magellan, with typical sea monsters seen in the Renaissance maps, and myself as the blowing wind (more appropriate than I like to admit). I also included a little poem within the oval border: 'My greatest self-discovery has been my DNA. A fractional inheritance from very far away. English, Irish, Portuguese, No. African, Malay. Gypsy out of India, and even Native A. Fully ⅛ African from down Cape Verde Bay. Wherever Portuguese explored lives in my genes today.'"

92 | Rug Hooking Journeys

*Going Places, 23½" x 17", #3- and 4-cut wool on linen.
Designed and hooked by Val Flannigan, Kelowna, British Columbia, 2017.*

"I have always been a fervent reader," Val said, "and over the last several years have become an ardent world traveler. Other than family, these are my passions in life. I find that whenever I read a fiction book, it takes me to another world. Sometimes I can even travel through time. I can learn about people I don't know and places I haven't been. I can read anywhere, and it takes my mind on an adventure.

"Traveling takes me physically on that adventure. I find that travel changes me. I appreciate my life. It broadens my mind and feeds my soul. It opens my eyes to ways of life that I would not otherwise know. In my life, both reading and traveling overlap in so many ways. They help me learn who I am. This rug was designed from a photo my husband took of me reading a book while we were traveling in Mendoza, Argentina."

Reflecting..., *30½" x 42", #3- to 7-cut hand-dyed and repurposed wool on cotton rug warp.*
Designed and hooked by Marilyn Becker, Wausau, Wisconsin, 2016.

Marilyn loves rug hooking and studying her genealogy, and this rug incorporates both passions. She is able to capture herself in the present looking back on her life as a child. The photo in this rug, shown right side up in the foreground and upside down in the mirror, is a family photo of Marilyn as a girl, feeding lambs.

In order to retain the detail in the family photo, she copied it onto fabric. "I couldn't hook them small enough to be clearly seen," she said. Marilyn hand-sewed the photos to the backing with polyester batting behind them, raising them to the height of the loops. This rug was featured in *Celebration of Hand-Hooked Rugs 27*.

Reflecting Again, *18″ x 22½″, #4- and 5-cut hand-dyed and repurposed wool on cotton rug warp. Designed and hooked by Marilyn Becker, Wausau, Wisconsin, 2017.*

"After I hooked my rug, *Reflecting . . .* ," Marilyn said, "I decided to see how far I could go with me looking at me looking at me. It was fun, but I think I have carried it as far as I can!"

Past, Present, and Future Selves | 95

Hooking Forward, 19″ x 21″, #3- to 7-cut wool, torn wool strips, silk, yarn, recycled fabric, and shirting strips on linen. Designed and hooked by Karen Greenfield, Elkhorn, Nebraska, 2018.

"This rug evolved out of a Deanne Fitzpatrick challenge, and then morphed into Heather Ritchie!" Karen said. "And I cut up one of my husband, Dixon's, good shirts for just the right shade of blue!"

On a trip with her husband to Solvang, California, Karen, who was born in Denmark, noticed an elderly Danish woman at a table in a Danish restaurant. The woman was clearly a regular at the restaurant. She knew her servers and conversed happily with them. She relished her simple meal of eggs and toast, with coffee and a beer. This woman was the initial inspiration for the figure in the rug, but, Karen said, "It's really me, sitting on the patio in my garden, hooking, and enjoying myself as much as that Danish woman in Solvang. In my rug design, I have removed all the neighbors. I call this rug *Hooking Forward*, because I used to live too much in the past. I can't change the past. So now I am looking forward and hooking forward."

Young Shepherdess, *35" x 49", #6-, 8-, 8.5-, and 9-cut wool on linen. Designed and hooked by Cathy Stephan, Athens, Wisconsin, 2018. This is an adaptation of the painting by Jean-Francois Millet.*

"I felt a connection to this girl," Cathy said, "because she reminds me of my life about 30 years ago as I was raising my children. I lived in a rural area with sheep flocks around at that time. We were gutting an old farmhouse and adding on to it, and with that work to do as well as gardening, canning, and raising the boys, I did not seek out activities or friendships. I spent a lot of time alone with my young kids around me, represented by the lambs around the girl. And I did a lot of thinking, pondering, and reading books, most of them of a spiritual nature. So I see her pondering life and meaning and God, which is what I was doing when young.

"I came to love things woolen, and learned to make rugs about 22 years ago. The girl is combing fleece into roving, which would later be spun into yarn. I did not spin roving but did come to love dyeing woolens and making rugs, clothes, and appliqué projects with it. It was the faraway look in her eyes that reminded me of that earlier time in my life."

Past, Present, and Future Selves | 97

CHAPTER VI
HOOKING TO HEAL

Back during our planning stages, we had no idea of including a chapter like this one. But as word got around, as ideas and concepts began to come in, as rug photos flowed into my inbox, we soon realized we had the contents of a new category of self-reflection rugs, namely rugs hooked as part of a healing process.

Healing from what? you may ask. Disappointment, disillusionment, criticism, social discomfort. The end of a relationship. The loss of someone dear. Physical restoration. Recovery from childhood trauma and psychic wounds. Creating such a rug may allow one to acknowledge and observe her own feelings in a calm and perhaps a somewhat detached way. The act of hooking the rug may help to give oneself empathy and support during a vulnerable time. Hooking to heal is an expression of compassion and understanding toward ourselves.

I applaud the rug hookers represented in this chapter, who have been willing to share not only their rugs—quite moving without explanation—but also their stories of disappointment, dark times, hurtful situations, and periods of debilitating grief. This chapter proves the words of Diane Cox: "Hooking is a meditative act of pulling fabric through a backing, and thus restoring yourself."

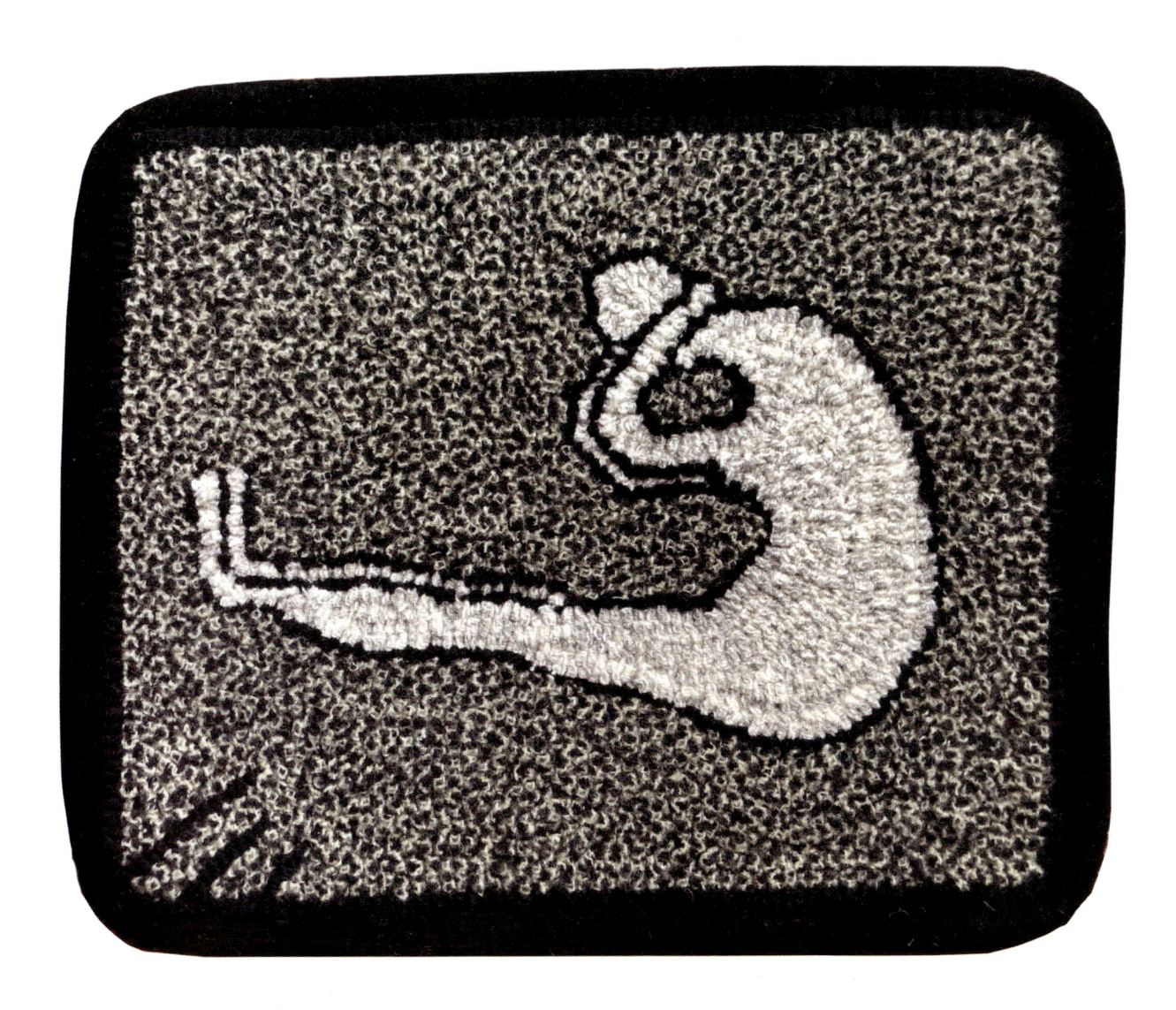

***Grief**, 11" x 9", #6-cut wool on linen. Designed and hooked by Sharon Townsend, Altoona, Iowa, 2015.*

The three black slashes in the lower left corner of this rug signify for Sharon the losses of her mother, her husband, and her daughter within six years' time.

Hooking to Heal | 99

My Heart Hangs Out to Dry, *30" x 54", recycled cotton tee shirts and thick knitting wools on hessian.
Designed and hooked by Sue Dove, Hayle, Cornwall, UK, 2012.*

    Sue developed this design from her painting of the same image. "In 2010, I initiated a divorce from my husband after a very long marriage," Sue said. "Although it was my decision, it was a difficult and emotional time, and I felt quite wrung out by it all. The rug is done in a naive style, and in fact it intrigues people who see it. I find it quite cathartic and compelling to use my life experiences and feelings in my work. The image of my heart hanging on a branch described my sense of detachment and also my need for time to recover from the hurt I was feeling."

My Heart Returns, *20″ x 70″, recycled tee shirts, thick knitting wool, and Sue's own mono-printed fabric on hessian. Designed and hooked by Sue Dove, Hayle, Cornwall, UK, 2014.*

This rug was translated from a painting that Sue had done. "I hooked this rug a couple of years after *My Heart Hangs Out to Dry*, when I began to feel better and had moved on emotionally. I created a small bird sitting on my shoulder, singing to me, reassuring and encouraging me, as nature often does. I felt it completed a difficult period in my life."

> "It is the way of the world that the night ends and the light returns. The light always returns."
> — Brian Andreas

Hooking to Heal | 101

Surviving Grief, *20" x 20", #4-cut wool on rug warp. Designed and hooked by Susan Jankowski, Neenah, Wisconsin, 2017.*

"I found myself draped in grief with the loss of a sister three years ago," Susan said, "and the sudden, shocking loss of two brothers last year, four months apart. My siblings were some of my best friends. I was just numbly trying to do the 'normal' activities, which included a hooking event in Milwaukee. At the end of that day, while walking into a quilt shop, I spotted this little pansy, surviving where you would never expect it, growing in a crack between a building and a driveway, so I took a picture. Later that night, as I was looking back at the pictures from that day, I saw the little flower again, and it dawned on me: I identified with this little flower, trying to survive, even flourish, while surrounded by cold, harsh conditions."

Aftermath, *26″ x 28″, #3- to 7-cut wool on linen. Designed and hooked by Diane Phillips, Fairport, New York, 2017.*

    After a period of painful disillusionment, Diane hooked this rug as evidence that she had not given up and was determined to carry on. "I was very angry and disillusioned at the time of the election," Diane said. "Friends would look at my rug and say 'you look angry.' I would say, 'I am angry.' Then they would ask, 'Why would you want to hook a rug where you look angry?' 'Because I AM angry,' I would reply. It is hard for some people to get over the notion that rugs must be pretty. Anyway, I believe that Americans are resilient and that ultimately we will come through for each other. I hope my rug also conveys that conviction. Hooking it was therapeutic." For the record, we find this rug beautiful, angry or not.

Hooking to Heal | 103

Rooted in Paisley, *12" x 16", #5- through 8-cut wool and antique paisley on linen. Designed and hooked by Anita White, Overland Park, Kansas, 2018.*

Anita was a runner for many years. Eventually, she transitioned to the gentler activity of yoga. "This self-reflection piece was created with inspiration for my love of antique paisley and my yoga practice," Anita said. "I chose tree pose because of the importance in having balance in my life. Being rooted, calm, and centered, and having acceptance of who I am is important to me. Hooking this piece also takes me back to the portrait that I hooked of my mother with a similar background."

The Misfit*, 16″ x 19″, #4-cut wool on linen. Designed and hooked by Lynn Goegan, Sturgeon Falls, Ontario, 2016.*

    Lynn always describes herself as a quirky person—and maybe that's exactly what makes her an artist. "My head is exploding," Lynn said of this rug, "and my colors are all coming out. The mice are my husband and me and our friends. I'm wearing a Bob Marley shirt, which is an inside joke in our family." Like every Lynn Goegan rug, the use of color is extraordinary here. One imagines that the feeling of being a "misfit" is not entirely happy. Yet making art from life is what artists do.

Hooking to Heal | 105

Saying Goodbye, 25" x 22¾", wool yarn, acrylic yarn, and a few loops of Mowgli's fur on linen.
Designed and hooked by Karen D. Miller, Ottawa, Ontario, Canada, 2017.

"I hooked *Saying Goodbye* when I was finally ready," Karen said, "five years after the passing of my cat, Mowgli. I based my design on a photo of one of our last moments together. He was lying in the yard where he had never been allowed when he was healthy, eating ice cream that he hadn't been allowed. It didn't matter anymore.

"Mowgli kept me company when I was alone, and he was with me through all of the studying and papers up to my graduations. He came along with the boxes for all of my moves, and he was the first member of my new family. Through all of the changes, he was always clearly and unconditionally my buddy, and I was his. I still smile when I think of his peculiar snort that used to emanate steadily from somewhere beneath my futon, how he somehow folded all of his fifteen pounds into the bathroom sink as though there was nowhere else in the apartment for a cat bed, and how he obligingly allowed my infant daughter to pull and tug at him while he tried to sleep.

"This was the moment I moved from never wanting him to go to accepting that he must. His life-ending illness was long and trying and, shortly after this moment, he died at home in my arms. I recognize that that pain was his final gift to me, because it came from our love that was so large. I think that it should be so with all of our relationships. Be kind. Love large. Never be forgotten."

Her Own Tears, 25″ x 35″ x 9″, #5- through 7-cut wool on linen, with hair and a metal bucket. Designed and hooked by Linda Rae Coughlin, Warren, New Jersey, 2013.

"For me," Linda wrote, "childhood to early adulthood was a time of never having enough. Not enough certainty, support, or love. How to handle this, that was the question. The option was to either drown in your own tears or keep your head above water. For a 'strong' woman, the choice is always easy; you must always keep your head above water!"

Hooking to Heal | 107

Stay/Leave, by Linda Rae Coughlin, Warren, New Jersey, 2007.

"This two-part set of luggage is more fact than fiction," Linda said. "The *Stay* piece is modeled after a distinct childhood memory. My father and his friend thought it was funny when they put a large, unfriendly dog in front of me and told both the dog and me to stay. If I moved, the dog would growl. Powerless and afraid, I learned a valuable lesson that day: Never, ever trust or be alone with that man. Years later, as a young woman, I was put to the test again. When it became clear it was time to leave a failed relationship, I was now in control of my situation. On no occasion would I let myself be put in a powerless position by an insecure man again.

"The red shoes/boots of both the child and the woman in each piece are symbols of self-confidence. Each piece is staged in a recycled suitcase. The *Stay* suitcase is packed with a stuffed toy. The *Leave* suitcase is packed with the man's Armani suit."

Stay Don't You Move, 20″ x 13″ x 12″, #4- through 7-cut wool on linen, with chains, appliqué, lace, and nylon. Designed and hooked by Linda Rae Coughlin, Warren, New Jersey, 2007.

Leave Now, 27″ x 18″ x 15″, #4- through 7-cut wool on linen, with appliqué and ribbon. Designed and hooked by Linda Rae Coughlin, Warren, New Jersey, 2007.

***Silent Whispers**, 14″ x 26″, #6- and 7-cut wool and hand-dyed recycled fabric on linen, with both digital and hand embroidery and metal butterflies. Designed and hooked by Linda Rae Coughlin, Warren, New Jersey, 2007.*

"This is one of seven pieces in a series of chakra healing pieces I am currently creating," Linda said. "This piece is for the fifth chakra, the throat chakra. The chakra color is turquoise, hence the color of the woman's skin. The three butterflies signify her transformation and spiritual evolution. The piece is a reminder that if one gets distressed with the words/actions of another, or by an upsetting situation, the following wellness practice can be applied. Reflect and notice why you are upset. Get quiet and say very little. Send loving kindness to both yourself and the offender/offended. Healing and being the best one can be: these are lifelong processes. With practice, this exercise can bring enormous well-being to both the wrongdoer and the offended."

Deliver Us from Evil, *43" x 31", hand-cut and #7-cut wool on linen. Designed and hooked by Linda Rae Coughlin, Warren, New Jersey, 2008.*

"In the wake of so many women breaking their silence about sexual harassment," Linda said, "I wanted to include this piece that I created a decade ago. It is about the sexual harassment I endured from a neighbor for ten years, until I moved out of my parents' house. This harassment was brought to the attention of the police, but because it was a different time, nothing was ever done to protect me or stop him." As Linda walked past the home of this neighbor, he exposed himself to her. When she changed her route, he found other ways to torment her. Linda lists many occupations in the "eyes" of the piece in order to show how this type of molestation can happen from unexpected people, in any circumstance. "This is not an easy memory for me to write about," Linda says, "but if it helps one woman find the strength to come forward, it is well worth it. It is gratifying to see that harassers are finally being held accountable."

CHAPTER VII

CREATING ALTER EGOS, CHARACTERS, AND HEROES

This is a chapter full of alternate selves, in which a maker has come up with a different version of her own identity. Though I keep trying to categorize them, they resist, which is probably a good indication that each rug deserves to be in a category all its own.

My alter-ego category contains the works of Loretta Scena, Sue Dove, Val Flannigan, Marsha Munter, and Brigitte Webb, who identify with a forest goddess, an angel, a mermaid, a flapper, and—a play on the word "hooker"—a lovely lady of the evening.

We have a small group of rugs inspired by art, in which Sue Dove adopts the look of Picasso, Loretta Scena offers her take on Klimt, and Lynn Goegan adapts a pictorial quilt design, all of which reflect versions of themselves. Dana Psoinas began with literature, the story of Little Red Riding Hood, turned upside down.

The caricature category includes Lynn Goegan's colorful *Me*, Karen Greenfield's achromatic *Matilde*, and Luci Bolding's *Lulu*, a grandmother tending her garden of grandchildren.

And finally, this chapter ends with my attempts to hook a desired state of mind, including several renderings of a favorite little character called Bea, who knows how to stop doing and just be.

Muireanne, 23½" x 17", #4-cut wool on linen. Designed and hooked by Val Flannigan, Kelowna, British Columbia, 2017.

"This piece was started in a class with Michelle Micarelli," Val said. "I have always wanted to design and hook a mermaid. I was inspired by the beta fish tails. The tail was great, but my drawing of her was not that glamorous. With Michelle's help, we gave her a tummy tuck and a breast lift. As a breast cancer survivor, I really related to this. She quickly became me and I made her hair long, flowing, and white. In the background water, I hooked small groups of fish in numbers of three, five, and seven, to represent my family members.

112 | Rug Hooking Journeys

Me, *14" x 14", #4-cut wool on linen. Designed and hooked by Lynn Goegan, Sturgeon Falls, Ontario, 2007.*

"An issue of *Rug Hooking* magazine came out, and I really admired Patty Yoder," Lynn said. "She had a self-portrait in that article. Of course, that made me want to hook one. I never make things the same on both sides, and this is the case with the glasses. I am a quirky person, so I hooked myself that way."

Sunny Day, *24" x 18", #4-cut wool on linen. Adapted with permission from a quilt, designed and hooked by Lynn Goegan, Sturgeon Falls, Ontario, 2015.*

"I loved this quilt," Lynn said, "so I obtained permission to hook it. I used to ride my bike around with my dog, Mr. Wilson, in my basket, so that might be why I identified with it. Also, how perfect are those sheep for a rug hooker? The sky was a lot of fun to hook."

Creating Alter Egos, Characters, and Heroes | 113

Welcome, 18" x 26", #3- to 6-cut wool, specialty yarn, and sparkle nylon material on rug warp. Designed and hooked by Brigitte Webb, Dingwall, Scotland, 2017.

"Janis Mennie, a well-known local artist, made a retirement card for me," Brigitte said, "and she was delighted to give me permission to adapt it to a hooked rug. This rug very much reflects my sense of humor. This design has to do with the fact that so many of our non-hooking friends introduce us to others as their hooker friend.

"My life partner photocopied the card and enlarged it to the size I wanted, which I then drew onto red dot and finally onto the rug warp backing. My wool stash was vastly depleted, so I held off starting until I returned from Nova Scotia—an unbelievable joy to return home with bulging suitcases. As usual, I struggled with hooking the face, but persistence paid off. I loved hooking the dress, but found the fishnet tights very hard to hook. A piece of fabric Judy Carter had once gifted me worked well for the glitter shoes. I used to dye my hair blond until my sister said not to bother, hence the blond here, but grey hair in my realistic portrait. In the background, I hooked a very small other self-portrait on the left side. It's me dressed as 'Maw Broon,' from when I took part in a gala with our local Woman's Institute group. This is one of my very favorite rugs."

"Be happy. It's one way of being wise."

– Sidonie-Gabrielle Colette

114 | Rug Hooking Journeys

***Matilde**, 17″ x 15″, #5-, 6-, and 7-cut wool on linen.
Designed and hooked by Karen Greenfield, Elkhorn, Nebraska, 2018.*

Karen has been using this little character, Matilde, as her signature for decades. She started with a simpler version, merely a face, drawn on the notes she put inside her children's lunch boxes. As she developed her business (creating home décor out of primitive antiques embellished with wool appliqué), Pretties and Primitives, Matilde showed up on the tags on Karen's merchandise. More recently, Matilde has acquired high heels, earrings, and thumbs up. Anyone who knows Karen can tell you that Matilde and she are one and the same. Karen used a charcoal gray (not pure black) and two slightly different shades of off-white in this rug, because Matilde is usually drawn on white paper.

Creating Alter Egos, Characters, and Heroes | 115

Lulu, 24½″ x 15″, #3-, 4-, and 6-cut wool on linen.
Designed and hooked by Luci Bolding, Omaha, Nebraska, 2017.

    Luci began this rug in a Donna Hrkman class. "I chose a caricature," Luci said, "because I had never done one before. I thought it would help me see myself in a fun way and not take myself too seriously. To challenge myself further, I chose a monochromatic color scheme. This was difficult as I only had five shades of turquoise to work with. I soon realized my heart was screaming for color. Hence, the flowers named for my grandchildren. Adding the color also brought clarity to the phrase, "You Color My World."

    "I learned through making this rug how expressing myself and sharing a part of me makes the rug more meaningful and makes it come alive. As I find myself in the grandmother phase of my life, I love to use rug hooking to share my life and my grandchildren with others. I realize how much fun I am having with them. In their own way, each child brings a different color to my world. I was blessed by this exercise."

The Guardian, 47" x 35", #3- and 4-cut spot-dyed, dip-dyed, casserole-dyed, and textured wool on linen. Designed and hooked by Dana Psoinas, Woodbury, New York, 2015.

The moment we set eyes on this award-winning rug, it seizes our attention. Not only does it put an interesting twist on the fairy tale of Little Red Riding Hood, it also suggests that overcoming fear can increase our personal power and potential. Dana Psoinas described her thoughts on this design in *Celebration 26*, but an event in her life has caused her to see *The Guardian* differently. "The meaning of this rug has evolved for me in very unexpected ways," Dana said. "Since my husband's car accident in September of 2016, it has come to represent my husband and me. We've always been each other's guardians through our life together, but my role had to become much more fierce during his stay in the hospital. I needed him to survive and return home to our family. We are both fiercely protective of each other."

Creating Alter Egos, Characters, and Heroes | 117

Veda of the Forest, 19½" x 24½", #3- and 4-cut wool, feathers, wool roving, appliqué, beads, ribbon, and specialty threads on linen. Designed and hooked by Loretta Scena, Deer Park, New York, 2018.

This rug is part of an Avatar series. "When I first drew Veda on the linen", Loretta said, "she was going to be a mask for a mask workshop that I was going to teach. From childhood, we use masks to dress up at parties and at Halloween, and they allow us to pretend to be something or someone different for a short time. An alter ego? Perhaps. But that's another story.

"As I hooked her, she began to evolve. She had qualities that I admire. She is a lover of nature. She cherishes the warmth of the sun on her skin, the song of the birds, the buzzing of the bees, the colors of the seasons and the scents in the air. She is strong. She faces obstacles and finds a way to overcome them and still have a pleasant smile. She is protective. No one would dare harm an animal in her presence, or damage the forest in any way without feeling her wrath. She is secretive. She is neither human, nor bird, nor leopard. She is the best and worst qualities of these species combined, and she would not be understood in society. She is kind. She knows that with love, anything is possible. She is magical and intuitive. She lets her senses guide her into being the best being she can be with the time she has been given."

"The name Veda comes from the Italian verb *vedere,* meaning 'to see.'"

***Water Serpents**, 33½" x 14½", #3-, 4- and 5-cut hand-dyed wool, beads, roving, gold lamé fabric, wool quillies, and selvedge flowers on linen. Adapted from a pattern by Melissa Pattacini of Honey Bee Hive Rug Hooking. Designed and hooked by Loretta Scena, Deer Park, New York, 2017.*

"This design is based on the art of Gustav Klimt," Loretta said. "I have always been an admirer of Klimt. His use of gold and a series of repetitive, colorful shapes in his artwork was both innovative and evocative. When I hooked this piece for a presentation at Northern Teachers Workshop, I chose to hook the leading lady with dark hair like mine. Is she a serpent? A mother? A lover? Is she me? Maybe, but it's more about the parts of me she represents that I wanted to put into this piece. As I go through the stages of my life, I think I have become more thankful and appreciative of my life and my creativity. I have always been happy that I am a woman. Sometimes while I hook, my thoughts are filled with memories of my experiences of being a mother, a lover, an artist, and a woman, for there are many different parts of self. As I hooked her, I enjoyed adorning her with colorful jewelry, embellishments, and designs. I think that Klimt himself would have admired my version of his wonderful painting."

Creating Alter Egos, Characters, and Heroes | 119

Dove and Dog Angel, *60" x 42", recycled cotton tee shirts, thick knitting wools, and vintage fabrics on hessian, with Sue's own mono-printed fabrics and hand embroidery. Designed and hooked by Sue Dove, Hayle, Cornwall, UK, 2015.*

"The idea behind this rug was all about how wonderful it would be to fly away sometimes," Sue said, "when life gets overwhelming, and to have the viewpoint of a bird! Of course, I could not possibly go anywhere without my beloved dog Frankie Velcro, Frank for short, who is a collie. But I always stylize my people and animals, as I prefer the look to a more realistic image. It gives the artist more freedom and allows her to give full flight to any ideas, yet it is still recognizable and resonates with the viewer. So I'm flying free through the skies with my dear dog, complete with wings. Hence the idea of us both being angels forevermore.

"The image comes, as all my work does, from a painting or paintings I always do first, to prepare for all my textile work. The small bird hanging down is 3-D and made by hand with stitch and embroidery."

"Making makes me believe in myself."
— Deanne Fitzpatrick

Dove and Dog Angel *(opposite page), detail.*

Sue's collage painting, the artwork that led to Dove and Dog Angel.

Creating Alter Egos, Characters, and Heroes | 121

The Reading Woman, *24" x 33", recycled cottons and chunky knitting yarn on hessian.*
Designed and hooked by Sue Dove, Hayle, Cornwall, UK, 2018.

"I consider this woman a version of myself, as all my rugs are. I see her as a suffragette. This rug was hooked to commemorate one hundred years since the partial introduction of votes for women, a subject that I am very interested in. In fact, I hope to do another rug based on the subject. I took inspiration from a Picasso painting, using the position of a woman in the Picasso. Picasso and Matisse are my favorite artists. I love their paintings of women and often go to them for inspiration. I create my own painting, then work the rug from my painting."

Sue embroidered the book cover. "If I used any wool, I cut it with scissors," Sue said. "I made the book and its subject quite subtle, so that the viewer discovers it while investigating the rug."

***Casandra**, 18" x 18" (cropped), #4-, 6-, and 8.5- cut wool on linen. Designed and hooked by Marsha Munter, Hickman, Nebraska, 2018.*

"This is a self-portrait of an imaginary Marsha Munter in the 1920s," Marsha wrote. "She lived her life as a flapper named Casandra. She loved to dress up in the vintage clothes and hang out in the salon where all the action was. She helped keep the salon entertained by singing, serving drinks, playing cards, and playing the piano for the locals and traveling guests. She loved the 1920s. They were the best years of her life."

Creating Alter Egos, Characters, and Heroes | 123

***The Bright Blessed Days**, 35" x 30", #6- and 8-cut wool, sari silk, and dyed seam binding on linen. Designed and hooked by Tamara Pavich, Council Bluffs, Iowa, 2017.*

"For a couple of years, I have been consciously hooking images that bring me peace. A connection with nature has always been soothing and nurturing for me. This ballerina has stopped dancing and has settled down to be one with her surroundings. All the orange flowers are blooming for her, and a bird has made a nest in her abundant hair. (I love birds.) The Louis Armstrong song 'What a Wonderful World' means a lot to me, so I named this rug for a phrase in the lyrics, 'the bright blessed days.'"

• •

*Right: **The Dark Sacred Nights**, 31" x 51½", #6- and 8-cut wool, sari silk, and dyed seam binding on linen. Designed and hooked by Tamara Pavich, Council Bluffs, Iowa, 2017.*

"After hooking *The Bright Blessed Days*, I had this idea about ballerinas. Not perfect ones, but regular, imperfect, human ballerinas, pursuing their art without regard for any audience, just for the joy of the dance. So I drew this rug for a Heather Ritchie class. Of course, with Heather, you get to try all kinds of fun techniques: her braids are made of braided strips of wool sewn down on the backing, the flowers (like creeping Jenny) are prodded, and her bosom is sculpted. The dark leaves of an oak tree are hanging above her, also proddy with some embellishment. It's a harvest moon, and the title of this piece is another scrap of lyric from 'What a Wonderful World.' Sometimes I need to stop doing and just be. So I named her Bea, and I have hooked versions of her in other rugs, too."

Creating Alter Egos, Characters, and Heroes | 125

***Fruits of the Spirit**, 14½" x 21½", #6- and 8-cut wool on linen.
Designed and hooked by Tamara Pavich, Council Bluffs, Iowa, 2018.*

"Here is Bea again. I hooked this rug on New Year's Day, to begin the year in the spirit of peace. In my family, we seem to measure our worth by our accomplishments, and this takes me out of balance sometimes. So while I hooked this simple, serene face and her basket of fruit, I thought about not trying so hard. 'Try softer,' a friend once told me. I believe in giving your best effort, but even the Apostle Paul omitted hard work from his list of the fruits of the spirit, which are love, joy, peace, patience, kindness, goodness, faithfulness, gentleness, and self-control."

126 | Rug Hooking Journeys

The Almost Virgin Queen, *34" x 40", #6-cut wool on linen. Designed and hooked by Pat Merikallio, Capitola, California, 2002.*

"I hooked this rug for the Green Mountain Rug Guild challenge of doing a nude self-portrait. There was no way I was going to hook a nude portrait of myself, so while walking through a library I saw a new biography of Queen Elizabeth the First and I had my 'Ah-ha!' moment. I put my face on her and gave her my scissors, hook, and bag. But, unhappily, the jewels are all hers."

CONCLUSION:
NAVIGATION TIPS FOR YOUR RUG HOOKING JOURNEY

This book is a catalogue of artists whose rug-hooking journeys have led them to their particular means of self-reflection. Every rug in these pages sheds light on its maker. Some of these works say simply, "here I am," or "this is me." Some elicit a chuckle, or perhaps a sigh over what might have been. Others are more opaque in their meaning, inviting further study or interpretation. Quite a few of these rugs may cause the viewer to think about her own identity, to apply the maker's idea or story onto her own life.

Having admired many of these courageous artists, how can we begin thinking about putting more of ourselves into our rug designs? Where to begin? Here are a few directions that you might travel on your Rug Hooking Journey.

Follow Your Bliss

One simple way to begin a self-reflective phase of your Rug Hooking Journey is to think of what makes you happy and make that the subject of your rug. For Val Flannigan, reading and travel give her great joy, and from these loves came her interesting design for *Going Places*. Val hooked herself in an easy chair, reading a book, with the continents of the big wide world spread across the background. For inspiration on Following Your Bliss, see Val's rug on page 93, or Anita White's *Rooted in Paisley* on page 104.

Follow Powerful Emotion

Happiness is only one of many strong feelings we experience. Others are anger, envy, sorrow, regret, grief, desire, excitement. We have placed Diane Phillips's rug, *Aftermath*, in our chapter called "Hooking to Heal", and yet, when we read her comments, we learn that she didn't really hook the rug to get rid of her anger, but rather to express her anger. Linda Rae Coughlin hooked *Her Own Tears* to convey a time in her youth when she didn't receive enough love or support. The design does nothing to assuage the sense of injustice of a child growing up with too little nurturing or protection, but rather it expresses perfectly Linda's emotions about that difficult time of life. For inspiration on Following Powerful Emotion, take another look at these works on pages 103 and 107, and also Sue Dove's *My Heart Hangs Out to Dry* on page 100.

Engage in Time Travel

Travel back to a period of great happiness or a time of intense pain, which by definition will have shaped who you are today. Hook that moment. Or travel ahead and anticipate the person you'll be in ten or twenty years. How has she changed, and how has she grown? For inspiration on Engaging in Time Travel, see Holly McMillan's *Good Old Holly* on page 85 and Diane Cox's *Bag Lady* on page 30.

Take the Whimsy Bypass

Let's leave seriousness behind and forget all rules about realistic portraiture. Think of what kind of person you are—let's say, someone who loves jewelry and high heels, and who has a positive attitude. That's enough. Now pick up a pencil and make a picture of yourself. This description happens to be a lot like Matilde, Karen Greenfield's happy little alter ego. Matilde is a chipper stick figure with hair bows, stilettos, pigtails, and thumbs up. Lynn Goegan captured her own identity with rosy cheeks, a necklace of jumbo pearls, unruly hair, and colorful lopsided spectacles. You can do this. For inspiration on whimsical self-reflection, see these rugs on pages 115 and 113.

Explore and Expand Your Identity

Have you ever looked in the mirror, hoping to be surprised for a change? If you've been seeing the same self for too long, it might be time to bust out of that identity groove. Maybe it's time to imagine the very opposite of who you think you are, and take a stab at hooking that interesting character. Say I've always been terribly sensible. I might imagine a self who's a bit reckless, one who says "the hell with it." One who dares to "go out in her slippers in the rain/And pick the flowers in other people's gardens/And learn to spit." For inspiration on Exploring and Expanding Your Identity, Google the poem "Warning" by Jenny Joseph, and see Brigitte Webb's *Welcome* on page 114.

Tune to Your Inner Voice

Sometimes life is filled with static. Chronic busyness, unrelenting obligations, the endless to-do list: all cause interference. I try to make my world smaller through self-reflective rug hooking. By drawing and hooking a serene being, I can emulate her serenity, quell the static in my own mind, and hear my own inner voice more clearly. For inspiration on Tuning to Your Inner Voice, see my *Bright Blessed Days* and *Dark Sacred Nights* on pages 124 and 125.

Travel with Friends

A like-minded rug-hooking friend can make a world of difference. Maybe you already have that friend who takes challenges with you, with whom you can try something new and compare notes. If not, be the one to reach out with an invitation to take the challenge of a self-reflective rug-hooking project. You don't have to live near your travel friends, either. Brigitte Webb of Dingwall, Scotland, is the only rug hooker in her town, and yet she has pen pals in the US, Canada, Britain, and even Norway, who are traveling with her on her rug-hooking journey.

Go Your Own Way

This Rug Hooking Journey is yours and no one else's. I wish you the courage to travel your own path in whatever direction you like and to share something of yourself through your art. You'll be giving me, and all your viewers, the singular pleasure of finding the maker in the rug.

SUGGESTED READING

American Hooked and Sewn Rugs: Folk Art Underfoot
Authors Joel and Kate Kopp are collectors and preservers of folk art, and their book is a favorite among rug hookers who value the history of the art. "The makers put something of themselves into these rugs through their intuitive artistry," the authors declare in their pithy introduction.

Barely Hooked
Rug hooking artist and gallery owner Rae Harrell's project collects rugs that depict the human form, with many self-portraits included in the volume.

Designed by You: Ideas and Inspiration for Rug Hookers
Tamara Pavich encourages rug hookers to draw inspiration from their own lives and design and hook the rugs that matter most to them.

Hooked Rug Portraits
Anne-Marie Littenberg wrote this definitive volume in 2011, and the chapters on studying faces, design, and self-portraits are especially relevant to this reading list. Published by *Rug Hooking* magazine.

The Illuminated Life: Your Third Age Lifebook
Professor Abe Arkoff wrote and self-published this helpful and enlightening book, which can be found with used booksellers online. Dr. Arkoff's book considers the later years of life to be "the third age," a time when we need to get our bearings again, reassess relationships, determine our third-age goals, and set a new course.

Inspired Rug Hooking: Turning Atlantic Canadian Life into Art
Almost any book by Deanne Fitzpatrick will teach us about expressing what we love in our rugs, but this book discusses creativity, passion, beauty, elements of design, and giving oneself permission to make art.

Mirror Mirror: Self-Portraits by Women Artists
Liz Rideal collects examples of the genre in many media. Delightful variety here.

On Women Turning 60: Embracing the Age of Fulfillment
Cathleen Rountree interviews twenty women about the experience of passing their sixtieth birthdays.

One Loop at a Time: A Story of Rug Hooking, Healing, and Creativity
Meryl Cook writes about the illness that put her on a path of healing and creativity.

Seeing Ourselves: Women's Self-Portraits
Beginning with the Sixteenth Century, Frances Borzello compiled this volume of self-portraits by female artists to demonstrate how they are quite different from the portraits that male artists make of themselves.

The Self-Esteem Workbook
Glenn R. Schiraldi, PhD, walks his readers through an interactive process of reading, pondering, and writing to change their habits of thought and become compassionate and kind to themselves. We include this book in our suggested readings for those who may be hooking to heal and for observers of changes in their lives and bodies.

Your Free Trial Of

RUG HOOKING MAGAZINE

Join the premium community for rug hookers! Claim your FREE, no-risk issue of *Rug Hooking* Magazine.

Sign up to receive your free trial issue (a $9.95 value).

Love the magazine? Simply pay the invoice for one full year (4 more issues for a total of 5).

Don't love the magazine? No problem! Keep the free issue as our special gift to you, and you owe absolutely nothing!

Get a Free No-Risk Issue

Claim Your FREE Trial Issue Today!

Call us toll-free to subscribe at (877) 297 - 0965
Canadian customers call (866) 375 - 8626
Use PROMO Code: **RRTY18**

Discover inspiration, techniques & patterns in every issue!

Yes! Rush my FREE issue of *Rug Hooking* Magazine and enter my subscription. If I love it, I'll simply pay the invoice for $34.95* USD for a one year subscription (4 more issues for a total of 5). If I'm not satisfied, I'll return the invoice marked "cancel" and owe absolutely nothing.

SEND NO MONEY NOW-WE'LL BILL YOU LATER

Cut out (or copy) this special coupon and mail to:
Rug Hooking Magazine Subscription Department
PO Box 2263, Williamsport, PA 17703-2263

First Name   Last Name

Postal Address   City   State/Province   Zip/Postal Code

Email Address

* Canadian subscribers add $5/year for S&H + taxes.
Please allow 6-8 weeks for delivery of the first issue.

RRTY18